D0777077

# SHAKESPEARE

# HOME STUDY BOOKS

HISTORY OF ENGLAND
By E. L. Woodward

RUSSIAN LITERATURE
By Richard Hare

BETWEEN THE WARS
By D. C. Somervell

LOCAL GOVERNMENT
By Arthur MacNalty

HOW TO RUN A SMALL FARM
By J. Gunston

A DIRECT ENTRY TO ORGANIC CHEMISTRY
By John Read

THE SOVIET WAY OF LIFE
By M. H. Lovell

THE ENGLISH LANGUAGE
By C. L. Wrenn

THE GREEK PHILOSOPHERS
By W. K. C. Guthrie

AN INTRODUCTION TO MODERN PSYCHOLOGY
By O. L. Zangwill

THE MICROPHYSICAL WORLD
By William Wilson

THE GROWTH OF THE ENGLISH NOVEL
By Richard Church

LATIN LITERATURE
By W. A. Laidlaw

WEST AFRICA
By F. J. Pedler

ANCIENT HISTORY
By Michael Grant

MEDIEVAL PHILOSOPHY
By Frederick C. Copleston

SHAKESPEARE
By Allardyce Nicoll

ENGLISH POETRY
By Douglas Bush

HOME STUDY BOOKS
General Editor: B. Ifor Evans

# SHAKESPEARE

by

ALLARDYCE
NICOLL

METHUEN & CO. LTD, LONDON
36 Essex Street, Strand, W.C.2

1952

*First published in 1952*

CATALOGUE NO. 4464/U

PRINTED IN GREAT BRITAIN

# CONTENTS

CHAPTER I

# THE BACKGROUND

DURING the last fifty years a vast cry of critics has swooped down on Shakespeare, and as a result the Shakespeare library, already by 1900 alarmingly extensive, has grown to mammoth proportions. Every year sees another yard-long shelf of volumes on the poet's life, his interests, his reading, his plays. Speculation runs riot and specialism rules. Perhaps the time is not far distant when certain scholars, instead of devoting themselves to Shakespeare's works generally, will restrict their attentions to single dramas. Even now it would take a man many years to become thoroughly conversant with the widely-flung literature on *Hamlet* or on *King Lear*.

For this critical activity there is ample justification. The sceptical twenties and thirties were sometimes inclined to regard the great flow of books and articles as merely part of 'The Shakespeare Industry', but of late we have been becoming more and more aware of 'The Shakespeare Wonder', of the unique position Shakespeare occupies in the world's literature. It is true that there are other authors, Homer and Dante for example, who have passed beyond the frontiers of place and time, and whose works give delight both to specialists and to ordinary readers; but not one of these other poets can claim such allegiance as Shakespeare does. During the three hundred years since his death he has not merely

1

retained his hold upon the English stage and continued to provide popular reading texts, he has also penetrated into the farthest reaches of the globe. The East celebrates his glories hardly less than the West. Beyond religion and politics he has moved serene. Amid the clash of modern ideologies his works are secure. Moscow and Warsaw join with his own London in paying tribute to his genius.

Not one other writer can claim the position he so confidently occupies. Men like Racine and Goethe and Schiller are, like Marlowe's kings, obeyed in their several provinces; only he is the true magician, godlike in his empery, with all things between the quiet poles at his command. To explain and to interpret this eminence demands that his work be scrutinized both minutely and from diverse points of view. Once and for all a lesser, yet still great, poet may be expounded in some brilliant critical volume: the excuse for the innumerable volumes on Shakespeare rests in the fact that the wonder which is in him defies exact description, that it constantly reveals fresh facets and that we can hardly imagine a time when we shall have exhausted the magic and become absolute masters of the mystery.

I

At the same time, when confronted with the enormous array of critics, jostling one another, stoutly testifying to their several beliefs, debating, contradicting, prophesying, we may feel prepared to put a despairing question: how can anyone hope, in the midst of these warring factions, to reach a reasoned judgement on Shakespeare's works?

There is not a single play which has not become

matter for fierce debate, and whole divisions of critics are arrayed in battle order, with dire threatenings trumpeting forth their challenge. Under one banner stand the historical critics, determined to regard Shakespeare only as an Elizabethan, a practising playwright serving up to naïve spectators what they wanted and not thinking in terms beyond the average of his age. Opposing them are the symbolists, whose Shakespeare is a mystic metaphysician, timeless and supreme, displaying a vision of basic truth. The former see *Hamlet* as a revenge play with many inconsistencies due to the inadequate assimilation of older material, and *Measure for Measure* as a kind of popularly moral fairy-tale; for the latter *Measure for Measure* takes shape as a profound Christian parable and *Hamlet* is a deeply considered whole, with symbolic connotations. Were this all, perhaps the problem would not be so serious, but, even within the serried ranks distinctions appear. During the past few years one of the symbolists finds that the Prince of Denmark is an image of death from whose presence the creatures of earth shrink shudderingly away, against whom they raise their pitiful hands in protest, while another symbolist views the same character as an image of essential life, miserably inhabiting a world of darkness and moral despair. For one critic Isabella's virtue is divine; for his companion that virtue is something rancid.

Besides these larger divisions other troops skirmish about, allying themselves now to one of the greater armies, now to the other. Some declare that Shakespeare belongs wholly to the stage, that only the actors may seek to interpret his lines and that nothing save what can be immediately appreciated by an audience is worthy of notice. In opposition are those who claim that essentially each one of his plays is a poem, the inner meaning of which can never be fully revealed during the quick traffic of the boards. Scenes which some look upon as spurious because supposedly puerile assume for others a peculiar splendour. This man sees Shakespeare as a Christian, and for that man naught is revealed save a profoundly pagan spirit.

The question with which we started may be repeated. When one book thus cancels out another, what prospect is there, for a reader who is not a specialist in this area, of fashioning an image of Shakespeare that shall not be a portrait dismally confused and lacking all authority? What has this enormous critical activity achieved save removing Shakespeare farther from us?

In seeking an answer to this question, we may as well admit frankly that so far little real attempt has been made at a synthesis of conflicting modern theories. Indeed, we may go even beyond that and confess that the number of these theories is so great and their conclusions so diverse as to make us wonder whether anything less than a great set of volumes could hope to make clear their complexity or could succeed to weave out of their variously coloured threads a comprehensive pattern. Nevertheless, despite these admissions, the fact remains that these variegated researches and speculations have carried us far towards a fuller understanding of Shakespeare's achievement and have largely been responsible for keeping him a living force in our midst.

From Shakespeare we are now removed by three and a half centuries, and the deep chronological abyss is paralleled by another abyss in thought. Since the days when Des Cartes set up a new philosophy the world has steadily, inexorably and destructively moved forward from scientific discovery to scientific discovery. The whole of life, physical and spiritual, has come to be dominated by the logical thought processes which have borne mankind from Newton's physics to the nuclear physics of the atomic age. The Elizabethan London of Shakespeare's days is separated from us, not simply as are Pope's London or the London of Byron by a lapse of time, but, much more significantly, by a completely different attitude towards the universe, towards nature and towards man. Unaided, we might well now have been unable to contemplate Shakespeare and his companions otherwise than as strangely yet colourfully clad men and women, viewed like mannequins in a museum and instinct with no more vitality than is possessed by wax figures staring fixedly at us with artificially glassy eyes.

Nor is this barrier, imposed by the prevalence of scientific thought, alone. When, some twenty odd years after Shakespeare died, the Puritans took control of England, tore down the maypoles, hacked down the Glastonbury thorn and executed a king, they did more than merely establish a short-lived Protectorate. They effectively set on the people of their own generation and on their descendants a harsh and rigid morality from the influence of which there has been but little escape. In good King Charles's golden days laughter returned for a spell for at least one section of the community, but this laughter was forced and sometimes echoed ominously against the unchanging wall of puritanic sentiment.

Ever since then England has been dominated, consciously or unconsciously, by the influence of the Revolution, thus separating itself off from the mood that inspired the sixteenth century. This was, of course, a world-wide phenomenon, but it affected England possibly more than certain other countries and we may not be wrong in thinking that some modern continental races, particularly the Latin, are, because still largely emotional, nearer in spirit to the Elizabethans than the people of England today.

Fortunately, within recent years, when the intellectual and spiritual cleavage might have banished Shakespeare as a living figure from our midst, many scholars have come forward to provide for us an understanding of his long-lost world. Not only have their efforts provided a counterbalance to the alien weight of scientific thought, it is not too much to say that, collectively, they have placed us in a position even more favourable to the securing of a true appreciation of the Elizabethans than any generation has had since Shakespeare's own time. In the interpretation of his works, the centuries immediately behind us moved darkly, sometimes by sheer intuition reaching a divination of truth but frequently falling into patent errors because in the interim so much that was commonplace to the sixteenth century had been completely forgotten. Now, we stand more securely. Although maybe we do not always make allowance for the disappearance of the Merry England of the past and are consequently inclined to disregard or refute flashes of insight on the part of certain continental critics, so many intimate studies have been made of diverse aspects of Elizabethan life, so many contemporary books have been minutely perused and so many documents carefully scrutinized, that we can readily, if we are prepared to permit our imagination free play, move back in time to live for a space in Elizabeth's London or to converse with the Stratford citizens of her reign. The knowledge at our disposal goes so far that, if we wished, we could make an almost complete house-to-house register of all the men and women resident in Shakespeare's birth-town for the years of his boyhood or for those of his retirement at New Place; it goes so far that without difficulty we may create in our fancy the average beliefs and aspirations of the time and assess by comparison with them the force of other less orthodox opinions held by small intellectual or sectarian groups. The 'Elizabethan World Picture' has been made familiar to us in books designed both for scholarly and popular reading.

It was a great age that Shakespeare lived in. Perhaps, were we enabled to visit it by the aid of some time machine, we should be shocked by many of its apparent crudities, but, if men of that time lived in constant apprehension of the plague, if an angry dagger's thrust might suddenly end their days, if their eyes were offended by the rotting heads stuck up to view on Tower Bridge, they had compensations a-plenty; we in our times have looked upon vast slaughter and incredible cruelties without comfort of the animating spirit which ruled then. And what deep spiritual force resided in the Elizabethan era is made immediately manifest by the manner in which it not only continues, even now, to exert a mighty spell upon us but also, as it were, seeps back and forward to claim areas not strictly belonging to it. In popular parlance a black-and-white timbered house built in 1450 will be styled 'Elizabethan', and even scholars writing of the Elizabethan drama are inclined to include everything which appeared on the stage up to 1640. Queen Elizabeth died in 1603, and, if we were to limit ourselves strictly, we should have to refuse the Elizabethan epithet to Shakespeare's greatest triumphs. *Hamlet* would just come in, but *Othello, Lear, Macbeth, Coriolanus, Antony and Cleopatra,* together with the final romances, would all lie outside the pale.

Despite such stretching of chronology, there is yet good reason for thus associating Elizabeth with the whole of the triumphant spirit expressed by Shakespeare and his fellows, and for embracing within this circle something at least which it inherited from the past and much of what it left as legacy for the future. Elizabethan England we now see as a period of extraordinary unity, symbolized in the person of the Queen herself. It was a unity in variety, not the unity dependent upon a drab level of uniformity. A vital democracy existed then, even although (perhaps even because) it was based on such a concept of 'degree' as was so potently expressed by Ulysses in *Troilus and Cressida.* England, the England which moves like an unseen hero through *Richard II,* suddenly assumed for all men a strangely moving spell. Norden and Stow and Camden explored its confines; Holinshed and Hall provided a richly-coloured record of its historical adventures; slightly later, Daniel and Drayton sang its wonders.

This England, too, discovered suddenly its own greatness. Drake and Raleigh carried its little ships over the vast oceans, and in 1588 the Invincible Armada foundered in watery ruin before the stalwart sailors and the winds of God which aided them. Although the greater part of the treasure of the Indies was passing into the power of Spain, some of these treasures too were being brought to English shores and, more importantly, the very concept of the New World, in the exploration and exploitation of which English voyagers were playing so important a part, was bringing to men's minds fancies rich and strange. 'Fancies' rather than 'thoughts'—because essentially the Elizabethans found their lives coloured, indeed shaped, by their emotions. We have only to read any one of the sonorous sermons of the time to recognize that thought does not follow thought in logical sequence but that emotional concepts burgeon out in luxuriant organic profusion. Instead of the exact exposition of an intellectual prose there is a richly imaginative flow of passionate words. These sermons are symbols of the time. This was not an age conducive to the encouraging of great philosophic inquiry. Men's minds tended to leap forward from passion to passion rather than from idea to idea.

For these men language became primarily an instrument for expressing emotional concepts, and as a consequence it did not require to be bound by the stricter, logical, rational rules which came to be imposed upon it just after Shakespeare's time. His syntax is typical rather than idiosyncratic, with emotional concepts governing the flow of words and often a complete disregard of formal sentence structure. Typical, too, is his obvious intoxication with words. For him and his companions language assumed the glory of a miracle; words became living things and there was a constant delight in observing their traits, in training them to do tricks, in listening to their bird-song or thrilling to their roar. Those puns which are so frequent in Shakespeare came to him from his age, for word-play of this kind is the result of an enthusiastic attention to sound and significance. When today we conventionally groan as a pun is uttered, we forget that we are unconsciously condemning ourselves: except for our poets, language has lost its living qualities, words have become counters and precise yet vague dictionary definitions have taken the place of subtle inferences.

Every Elizabethan poet and prose-writer was a word-creator, one fetching his trophies from the ancient classical tongues, another unearthing long-forgotten medieval terms, another quarrying in French and Italian mines, still another boldly inventing fresh combinations of sounds to fit fresh concepts. No dictionaries fettered words to the shackles of precise meanings; no grammars imposed heavy rules of behaviour. For the poets, no doubt, the excitement was most intense, but all shared in the current passion. We have but to think of Costard in *Love's Labour's Lost*. Don Armado has just given him some money as remuneration for services rendered. 'Now', says Costard, opening his hand and glancing at the coins,

> will I look to his remuneration. Remuneration! O, that's the Latin word for three farthings: three farthings—remuneration. 'What's the price of this inkle?'—'One penny.'—'No, I'll give you a remuneration.' Why, it carries it.—Remuneration!—why it is a fairer name than French crown. I will never buy and sell out of this word.

The acquisition of a new term, for Costard as for others, was of greater worth than material possessions. If we want another example we need go no further than Shallow in *Henry IV*. Bardolph has just addressed him:

> Sir, pardon; a soldier is better accommodated than with a wife.

Immediately Shallow's excitement becomes obvious:

> It is well said, in faith, sir; and it is well said indeed too. 'Better accommodated!' It is good; yea, indeed, is it: good phrases are surely, and ever were, very commendable. 'Accommodated'! It comes of 'accommodo'; very good; a good phrase.

The savouring of the word is as the savouring of a connoisseur, even although Shallow makes no literary pretensions.

Words are means of expressing emotions, and both words and emotions belong to men. In men, in men's passions and in men's personalities, the Elizabethans were deeply interested. This interest was general, but it was particularly focused on two things—the qualities that made certain men soar a pitch beyond their companions and the qualities that brought men of otherwise diverse births and attainments under single banners. Adopting and adapting the medieval concept of the humours, they vigorously explored the reaches of the choleric type, the phlegmatic, the sanguine, the melancholic. They wanted to know what made men merry or sad; they sought to determine why these men were even-tempered, why those were irascible or inclined towards gloom. Nor was their interest restricted, as our modern psychological studies so frequently are, to the scrutiny of the individual. They were socially minded and they believed in a society of ordered parts, whereof the consecrated monarch was the head: consequently, they were continually intent upon examining the relationship between the ruler and the ruled, the qualities demanded of a good and capable king, the interrelations between the various social groups of which the entire society was composed. Still further, to the interest in man related to other men—the political aspect—was united an interest in man related to God —the religious aspect.

There is one obvious deduction here. For the Elizabethans, with these interests, the drama was the art best fitted to express their deepest and innermost convictions, the art most fully designed to appeal to the people. Poetry could give much, prose pamphlets, some of them approaching the novel in form, abounded, but in neither was there the opportunity of watching men and women, as though in life, acting out their stories upon the stage and directly expressing themselves in richly sounding words.

II

The true significance of the Elizabethan theatre is another subject whose scope has first been revealed to us by the investigators of the last fifty years.

In the year 1576 the hitherto wandering actors, who had had to satisfy themselves with trestle stages set up in inn-yards and elsewhere, found themselves sufficiently prosperous to be able to erect for themselves a permanent home—The Theatre, in Shoreditch. By lucky chance or by careful planning (as one may reasonably speculate since the actors were practical and by then experienced men), the play-house was designed in such a way as to offer the fullest opportunities for dramatists and performers. Every-one now is familiar with the main features of this playhouse—its large round auditorium open to the sky, its platform jutting out into the middle of the yard, its inner stage, concealed when need be by a curtain, its balcony set in the façade before which the action was presented: but few perhaps stop to con-sider how perfectly adapted this stage was for Shakespeare and his contemporaries or how much it might have been the envy of less happier lands.

A comparison of Renaissance Italy with Renaissance England in this respect will serve to demonstrate the virtues of the Elizabethan theatre. From the time of Ariosto onwards Italy engaged as actively as did England in stage affairs, yet hardly one of those many tragedies and comedies produced by her poets is read today by any save specialist students. The cause of failure may well be traced to the fact that in Italy there were two distinct kinds of play-house and play—the *commedia erudita*, the 'erudite' or literary drama performed, mostly by amateurs, in elaborate ducal theatres with rich scenic and machine effects, and the *commedia dell' arte*, the play of the professional actors, a thing largely of improvisation owning to no authors, performed on rude trestle stages set up as occasion demanded in town square or castle courtyard. In the former productions the dull wit of the learned amateur was accompanied by visual wonders; in the latter the native wit of the actors was ill put forth and lacked refinement.

In Shakespeare's England the 'University Wits'— Greene and Marlowe and Kyd—applied themselves

to providing material not for the amateurs but for
the professional players, and the stage of those professional players was neither so gaudily rich as the
private theatres of Italy nor so barely simple as the
hastily assembled platforms on which Harlequin and
Pantaloon disported themselves. Here, in The
Theatre of 1576 and in those later theatres built on
the same model, including Shakespeare's The Globe,
was a broad stage well suited both for the enunciation of rich words and for rapid movement, accompanied by such devices as the inner and upper stages
for diversity of display: here the money that in Italy
was expended on scenery was laid out in expensive
costumes, so that the eye, instead of being confronted
by a colourful background, was directed towards the
actors. In The Theatre and The Globe, with the
moving panoply of handsomely dressed players
moving against a simple unchanging background,
scenery became dynamic and integral in place of
remaining static and incidental.

The conventions born of this playhouse are, like
its shape, fairly well known; some of them need not
trouble the general reader of Elizabethan dramatic
works but others, affecting the essential structure of
these works, must be held constantly in mind. In
particular, the fact has to be remembered that this
theatre ever summoned forth the imagination of the
spectators and made these spectators part creators of
the theatrical performance. When we read Shakespeare's plays in a modern edition with precise indications of locality inserted by the editors, we do
Shakespeare wrong—partly because we are thus led
to give a local habitation and a name to what was
conceived as nameless and vague, and partly because

the exact indication of place, with the consequent separation of the play into scenic units, causes us to lose the effect secured by flow from action to action. In reading or in producing a Shakespearian comedy or tragedy we should pause hardly for a moment. Scene after scene might be cited to demonstrate that the dramatist sought to secure his effects not only by contrast of character with character, by continual interplay of phrase and phrase, but no less potently by sharp contrast of scene with scene: and to appreciate his subtlety we require to read and see his works in terms of the theatre that offered him the opportunity and for which he wrought his action.

In considering Shakespeare's relationship to his theatre and to his age, we must bear in mind the peculiarly fortunate time of his birth. The great writer does not owe his greatness to the precise era in which he lives, but to that era he certainly owes the opportunities given him for the cultivation and free expression of his genius: and, since time moves subtly and swiftly, a few years' difference may make or mar his work. It is not too much to say that, had Shakespeare been born a decade earlier or a decade later, such opportunities would have been denied him.

Sometimes, in speaking of Elizabethan literature, we are apt to forget that the first twenty-five years of the Queen's reign did not produce much of peculiar excellence. The great surge of poetry and prose which we associate with her was not truly prophesied until the eighties of the sixteenth century and did not reach fulfilment until the nineties. In the world of the theatre John Lyly was experimenting with his romantic comedy as early as 1584, but his best-known plays come between 1588 and 1594.

Robert Greene's *Friar Bacon and Friar Bungay* did not appear until about 1589, Christopher Marlowe's *Tamburlaine* belongs to 1587, Thomas Kyd's *The Spanish Tragedy* to 1589. Until the late eighties the stage was largely possessed by the 'jigging veins of rhyming mother-wits and such conceits as clownage keeps in pay'.

In 1589 Shakespeare was twenty-five years old, just of the right age to apply himself to the stage. A dramatist, unlike a lyrical poet, needs to have some maturity before he can succeed in his craft, for the drama is a thing not merely of words but also of characters. Shakespeare's finest works did not come until he was in his late thirties and forties. If he had been born in 1554 instead of 1564 he would have been compelled to devote his precious early years to toilsome pioneering, instead of arriving at the theatre's doors when Lyly had fashioned a novel form of romantic comedy, when Kyd had developed a new pattern of tragic complication and, above all, when Marlowe had shaped a vigorous blank-verse style and had introduced wonder to the stage. Had he been born in 1574, he would have reached London long after the first excitement of the new style had lost its gloss; instead of being inspired to explore the ranges of a freshly discovered and partly untried instrument, he would have been dominated and fettered by the cadences and by the themes of his predecessors.

The same is true of his relation to the Elizabethan playhouse itself. In 1590 this theatre was still something of a novelty, its gloss unimpaired and its full potentialities unexplored. By the beginning of the seventeenth century men were beginning, in a broad and restless way, to dream of a different kind of play-house, but for the young Shakespeare in the nineties there was constant excitement in learning the stops of this as yet largely untried instrument. Once more the date of his birth in 1564 was peculiarly fortunate.

### III

The manner in which recent investigations of the Elizabethan era and of the Elizabethan stage have brought Shakespeare near to us is paralleled by our indebtedness to those who have specialized in bibliographical research.

For a non-specialist reader of Shakespeare it may seem strange, and perhaps foolish, that after the long array of editions of his works stretching back to the famous First Folio of 1623 there should still be scholars devoting their entire lives to the preparation of yet other editions. Definitive texts of other poets' work have been issued: why therefore should there be the need for new editions of Shakespeare?

The question, a valid one, is answered by the facts that only within the past thirty years have we been enabled to gain an accurate knowledge concerning printing conditions in the sixteenth century, that even now new discoveries are being made and that not all of the plays have been as yet fully examined in the light of these new discoveries.

Obviously, what we all want to have for reading is a text of Shakespeare which shall be as close as possible to the poet's original manuscript. This means that, if we find two printings of a particular play each with its own variants, we need to decide how these variants came into being: in other words, we want to get behind the printed text and determine what was the 'copy' from which the compositor set up his lines. Before the bibliographical studies of the past few years the basic facts were unattainable, or conclusions were arrived at which were completely at variance with what we now know to be the true facts. A couple of examples will make this clear.

About half of Shakespeare's plays appeared during his lifetime as separate quartos. Among these quartos there are two, quite distinct, of *A Midsummer Night's Dream*, both with the year 1600 on the title page. In the past there was a good deal of inconclusive argument designed to prove that one or the other of these was the genuine 'first' and according to their particular predilections various editors gave preference to readings now from this quarto and now from that. It was not until 1917 that precise evidence was given proving that one of these quartos had actually been set up, not in 1600, but in 1619 and that therefore its variations could be of little account.

The second example concerns the second part of *Henry VI*. This appeared first in the collected Folio of 1623, but in 1594 there had been issued a quarto entitled *The First Part of the Contention between the Two Famous Houses of York and Lancaster*. Although the quarto differed materially from the Shakespearian *Henry VI, Part 2*, the two texts were clearly connected, and, since the former was manifestly weaker, all scholars had assumed that *The First Part of the Contention* was either an unrevised original of the other play or else the basis on which it had been founded. From these deductions all kinds of theories were established concerning Shakespeare's early workmanship, some critics discussing the way in which the poet improved on the writings of his predecessors, others speculating on the manner in which he revised his own juvenile work. In 1924, however, it was almost conclusively proved that this *First Part of the Contention* is nothing more than a corrupt and 'pirated' version of the Folio's *Henry VI, Part 2*. So far from having before us an interesting early drama here, we are confronted only by a bad text.

The discovery that several of the early quartos, so far from being 'source-plays', are simply bad versions of dramas which have elsewhere been preserved in good texts, is one of the most important achievements of modern bibliography, going alongside of the complementary discovery that others among the quartos are texts so good that they may well have come directly from Shakespeare's own manuscript. In Elizabethan times, it has been found, the author sold his play outright to the acting company, and in general the company was not eager to see the contents of its repertoire reproduced in print. The play manuscripts were precious things, to be guarded carefully lest other troupes, in the absence of adequate copyright provision, seized upon them. These conditions made piracy of new and popular dramas a profitable business, and some disreputable publishers were only too ready to come to terms with minor actors and others capable of producing something at least approaching the original text. Naturally, such pirated versions were botched affairs, often deviating so far from the authoritative copy as to make them seem to be independent works. On the other hand, when the acting company was compelled (because of the need of ready money, or because of the author's insistence) to authorize the publication of a 'good' quarto, we now know that the manuscript provided for the compositor was likely to have been either in the author's own hand or in a hand which had transferred his lines directly on to a fair copy.

The foundation, accordingly, is being laid for a more exact determination of what Shakespeare actually wrote and for the making of reasonable deductions concerning passages in his manuscript where the poet has revised earlier lines or added to the already existing text. Since these bibliographical researches have gone alongside a more meticulous exploration of the meanings attached to words in Elizabethan times, a cautious conservatism animates most of modern editors. Perhaps the ideal has as yet not been reached in practice, but at any rate the ideal has been expressed—to determine, where possible, the words as they stood in Shakespeare's copy and not to be misled into making emendations until it is certain that no valid significance can be worried out of phrases apparently obscure. The result is that many emendations suggested by earlier editors have been rejected and the Elizabethan text restored, and such a process of readjustment is still proceeding. Quite recently, for example, a continental scholar has shown, by reference to Elizabethan beliefs in the supernatural, that the original Folio reading of 'rebellious dead' ought to be replaced in *Macbeth* instead of the emendation 'rebellion's head' hitherto accepted by almost all editors. When Macbeth declares:

That will never be.
Who can impress the forest, bid the tree
Unfix his earth-bound root? Sweet bodements, good!
Rebellious dead rise never till the Wood
Of Birnam rise——

the words, properly understood, create an imaginative picture entirely lost when the flat 'rebellion's head' is substituted.

This does not mean, of course, that emendation in numerous scenes is not necessary. Elizabethan compositors were not always as careful as they should have been, and unquestionably there are passages in the 'good' quartos and in the Folio which cannot possibly represent what Shakespeare wrote. Where such emendation has to be introduced, however, modern scholarship categorically rejects the wild guessing in which the earlier editors indulged so gaily. The demand is now made that any changes must be made explainable in terms of Elizabethan handwriting; it is now incumbent upon an editor setting forth any new reading to show that the word he proposes would have assumed such a form in Shakespeare's manuscript as to have caused a compositor to mistake it for the word he set up in type.

Beyond even this have modern editors gone. In the past, the punctuation of the quartos and the Folio was disregarded as something incomprehensible and confusing. Recent studies, however, have demonstrated that, although commas and semicolons were used in the sixteenth century with nothing like the exact precision imposed on us by our modern grammars, there was a kind of rhetorical system in use. As a result of the recognition of this fact, scholars are beginning to see, in the punctuation of several plays in the 'good' quartos and in the Folio, signs of Shakespeare's guiding hand at work. Perhaps at times too much is made of this, and certainly the enthusiastic application of the term 'beautiful' to the placing of some comma or other must be deemed exaggerated, but the fact remains that this discovery too is leading us closer to an appreciation of Shakespeare's intention, is carrying us beyond the printing house back into his study.

New aspects of these problems are continually being exposed. A good example here is the lineation of Shakespeare's verse. The base of this verse is, of course, the decasyllabic line, the line of normally five stresses and ten syllables. In the original texts such lines are by no means regular: sometimes passages obviously intended as blank verse are printed as prose and in other passages the normal lines are broken up on the page. Quite naturally, editors have been in the habit, when confronted by such broken lines, of trying to restore a regular lineation, on the assumption that Shakespeare, since he was penning lines in the blank-verse rhythm, must have intended these lines to take form in a set pattern. We turn, for instance, to the scene in *Macbeth* after the murder, which thus appears in the Folio text:

*Enter Lady*

*Lady.* My Hands are of your colour: but I shame
To weare a Heart so white. *Knocke.*
I heare a knocking at the South entry:
Retyre we to our Chamber:
A little Water cleares vs of this deed.
How easie is it then? your Constancie
Hath left you vnattended. *Knocke.*
Hearke, more knocking.
Get on your Night-Gowne, least occasion call vs,
And shew vs to be Watchers: be not lost
So poorely in your thoughts.

*Macb*. To know my deed,                    *Knocke*.
'Twere best not know my selfe.
Wake *Duncan* with thy knocking:
I would thou could'st.                    *Exeunt*.

It is entirely understandable that in nearly all modern editions these lines should be regularized thus:

### Re-enter *LADY MACBETH*

*Lady Macbeth*. My hands are of your colour; but I shame
  To wear a heart so white. (*Knocking within*.) I hear a
    knocking
  At the south entry: retire we to our chamber:
  A little water clears us of this deed:
  How easy is it then! Your constancy
  Hath left you unattended.          (*Knocking within*.
                    Hark! more knocking:
  Get on your nightgown, lest occasion call us
  And show us to be watchers: be not lost
  So poorly in your thoughts.
*Macbeth*. To know my deed, 'twere best not know
  myself.                    (*Knocking within*.
  Wake Duncan with thy knocking!  I would thou
    couldst!                    (*Exeunt*.

The words are precisely the same, but of late it has been acutely pointed out that the modern text dissipates all the dramatic tension in the original lines, that Shakespeare probably wrote the speeches as they appear in the Folio text, and that he seems to have been deliberately making theatrical use of breaks in the regular pattern. Lady Macbeth starts with a line and a half in formal blank verse. The knocking interrupts her and in a rush comes, 'I heare a knocking at the South entry', followed by a sharp command, uttered, as it were, outside the blank verse cadence. Then she recovers herself. From 'A little water' down to 'unattended' the blank-verse rhythm is recaptured—only to be broken again by the repeated knocking. After a pause, she steels herself to enunciate two and a half lines of regular verse, and Macbeth begins to complete the last of these lines when the third knocking shatters his assurance. The anxious pause is followed by two sharply truncated lines:

> 'Twere best not know my selfe.
> Wake *Duncan* with thy knocking—

and, after another pause, by the despairing:

> I would thou could'st.

There seems to be no doubt about it: any sensitive reader must agree that reading the lines in the modern text produces a different, and a vastly inferior, emotional effect from what is produced by the lines in the Folio. This is something which is not just a matter for the meditation of scholars but is of vital importance for the reader or actor intent on appreciating the spirit in which Shakespeare conceived his scene and intended it to be interpreted on the stage.

Perhaps sufficient here has been said both to indicate the debt we owe to the modern bibliographers and to show why the editing of Shakespeare is as yet an incompleted task. No doubt some day we shall reach such a final text as the available evidence allows us to reconstruct. But, even as it is, we may say with assurance that today's reader is immeasurably nearer to what Shakespeare originally wrote than any readers from his own time to ours.

Beyond the importance of these studies for determining the text, however, the information we have gained concerning the composition and sale of plays, the relationship between the author and the printer, the inner working of the printers' establishments and the conditions operative in the publishing trade, has thrown further light on the way in which Shakespeare wrote. The absence of effective copyright, at least in so far as dramatic works were concerned, had many implications, and among them not least is the frequently forgotten fact that, while it resulted in the publication of the many 'bad' quartos, it permitted freer scope to Shakespeare than he could have had if he had lived in our own days. Its absence means not only that authors were allowed to refashion the perhaps unsatisfactory writings of their predecessors, but also that the modern concept of plagiarism was virtually non-existent. Shakespeare's *Hamlet* probably could not have been penned had the Elizabethans possessed such a copyright system as rules in the twentieth century. At least as early as 1589 we hear of a *Hamlet* on the stage and most scholars believe its author was Thomas Kyd. If so, then Shakespeare's tragedy of 1601 was no doubt built directly on the earlier work, just as his *King John* is generally thought to have been a reworking, virtually scene by scene, of an older two-part drama on that monarch's reign. To reach anything that might be parallel in our own times we should have to imagine a young playwright being allowed, without the danger either of legal injunction or of public criticism, to take Shaw's *Saint Joan*, to follow its action step by step, to rewrite the dialogue (although retaining some lines of the original), to build up already existing characters, to introduce other persons not appearing in Shaw's drama, and to bring the new play forward under his own name without any acknowledgement to G.B.S. No doubt copyright laws are necessary and desirable in order to protect dramatic authors: but *Hamlets* are now impossible.

Much more significant, although less fully observed or appreciated, is the spiritual climate resultant from the lack of the idea of plagiarism. Today a young author approaches the theatre with a sense of fear. It is not that he is afraid lest an action be brought against him for infringement of copyright: after all, this is a comparatively infrequent occurrence. What is unconsciously imposed upon him is the necessity to be original in his plot, to devise novel situations, to invent his story. Of such invention in Elizabethan times there was little. All but one or two of Shakespeare's plays can be traced back directly to an original tale or historical narrative. He did not need to invent in this way, nor did his audience expect him to do so; and the result was that his mind was freed for the vastly more important task of fashioning character and, particularly, of conceiving fitting words for his borrowed action. The Elizabethan audience was sufficiently naïve, and sensible, to be content with familiar stories made vital by a poet's words, to recognize that novelty in plot invention brings merely a passing thrill and that what gives permanent strength in the theatre is a combination of vigorous interpretation in human terms of perhaps well-known actions and of words so fitted to the characters that they seem inevitable.

# CHAPTER II

# THE PROBLEM OF INTERPRETATION

OUR indebtedness to the scholars who have thus revealed the temper of the Elizabethan age and who have brought us nearer to the words originally set on paper by Shakespeare is incontrovertible. No doubt arises here: we are confident that their researches have indeed brought us back over the wastes of time to the threshold of Elizabeth's London.

What, however, are we to say of the diverse, conflicting views expressed regarding Shakespeare's work as a whole and regarding particular plays by the enormous throngs of critic-interpreters?

I

In approaching this vast area of Shakespearian criticism we must be cautious and above all we need some guiding principles. And here, perhaps, the eighteenth century, if it fails us when we seek for information on Elizabethan England, may give us some guide.

Two concepts animate the greater part of Shakespearian criticism during the eighteenth century—Nature and Good Sense. Shakespeare was Nature, or at least a Child of Nature, and Good Sense, or Common Sense, ruled in his works and in his actions. 'The latter part of his life', remarks his first biographer, Nicholas Rowe, in 1709, 'was spent, as all men of good sense will wish their's may be, in ease, retirement and the conversation of his friends.' Later in 1769 David Garrick lilted:

There never was seen such a creature;
Of all she was worth, he robb'd Nature.
He took all her smiles, and he took all her grief—
And the thief of all thieves was a Warwickshire thief,
    Warwickshire thief,
      He's the chief,
For the thief of all thieves was a Warwickshire thief.

Common Sense and Nature. At first glance, perhaps, we might feel prepared to dismiss the one as merely a reflection of that which this Augustan age set before itself as an ideal and the other as partly a critical cliché, partly an attempt to find excuse for a poet, obviously great, who yet contravened all the best 'rules' of exact literary composition.

Maybe, however, the significance of these two concepts goes much deeper than we might imagine. It is interesting to observe that during recent years several critics have come to recognize the profound acumen expressed in the Shakespearian criticisms of Dr. Johnson, the very high-priest of eighteenth-century good sense, and, when we look at the matter carefully, we are led to believe that this acumen derives from the fact that here a man of good sense discovered his kinship with one who basically was the quintessence of common sense, that here a man of broad interests met a peer of nature.

After all, when everything has been said, is not level-headedness the quality which impresses us most strongly in Shakespeare? Sometimes we call this the enigma of Shakespeare, yet if it is an enigma its qualities are simple. It gives us a feeling of safety in his company. Most poets are, because intoxicating, a trifle dangerous: they are doctrinaire because self-centred; and even with the best of them we must

remain on our guard. From their lips issue forth such
siren melodies we risk being drawn within their
charmed circle; we know that, were we to permit
ourselves completely to be enchanted, our view of life
might well become one-sided and imperfect, a frail
image of the poets' own self-centredness. It is not
only the Shelleys and the Byrons about whom clings
this tremor of danger, it is present even in the Miltons
and the Wordsworths. The mien of all of them is
serious: to admit a smile at their own passionate
enthusiasms would dissipate their virtue.

Shakespeare is always ready to smile at himself,
and, unless we appreciate this cardinal quality and
unless we come to him in the light of double vision,
we shall at once be unable to understand his works
and be forced to abandon search for the springs of
his greatness. The failure of many critics, and perhaps particularly the critics of our own century, lies
in the fact that they approach in a doctrinaire and
over-serious manner one who was farthest from the
doctrinaire spirit and from whom quizzically raised
eyebrows are more to be expected than a frown.
Nearly all that Shakespeare had to give was poured
into the mould of dramatic art, yet it was he who
wrote: 'The best in this kind are but shadows, and
the worst are no worse if imagination amend 'em.'

At moments we believe that we have caught him.
When Berowne speaks in *Love's Labour's Lost*, we say
confidently, there is the voice of the young poet,
contemptuous of dull learning:

> Small have continual plodders ever won,
> Save base authority from others' books.

That indeed sounds as though it were a personal

expression of opinion coming from a youth conscious of his own creative imagination and bored with the world of scholarship. Yet let us scan the next few lines of the scene. Almost immediately after Berowne's ecstatic praise of ladies' eyes and his carefully balanced rhetoric,

> How well he's read, to reason against reading!

says the King, and Berowne's bubble is burst. In *As You Like It* we are introduced to a highly patterned piece of lyrical dialogue, wherein Rosalind, Phebe and their companions indulge in a love chant: so mannered are the lines, so artificial, we may for a moment allow ourselves to smile superiorly and indulgently at the author's artificiality, but the smile is wiped from our lips when we listen to Rosalind's comment:

> Pray you, no more of this: 'tis like the howling of Irish wolves against the moon.

In blank verse Shakespeare found the supreme instrument for the expression of the melodies within him, yet when Orlando greets Rosalind with a

> Good-day and happiness, dear Rosalind!

Jaques comment is instinct with Shakespeare's smile:

> Nay, then, God buy you, an you talk in blank verse.

The joys of the greenwood are highly praised by the exiled Duke:

> Now, my co-mates and brothers in exile,
> Hath not old custom made this life more sweet
> Than that of painted pomp? Are not these woods
> More free from peril than the envious court? . . .

> . . . This our life exempt from public haunt
> Finds tongues in trees, books in the running brooks,
> Sermons in stones and good in everything.

No one better than Shakespeare, however, knew the prickly discomforts of the forest, and his Duke at the end is only too anxious to seize on 'the good' of 'our returned fortune', when fate permits him to return to court.

Throughout almost the whole of Shakespeare's work this quality has an enduring force. We are laughing with the courtiers of *Love's Labour's Lost* at the absurd antics of the Worthies, but Holofernes' rebuke:

> This is not generous, not gentle, not humble,

is addressed at us, and at the creative poet himself, as at the witty young gallants. Don John's plot in *Much Ado About Nothing*, which almost tragically hoodwinks Claudio and the rest of the delicately nurtured and finely cultivated gentlemen, is destroyed by none save the ludicrous, blundering Dogberry. In the more serious plays this quality becomes transmuted into something richer still and penetrates to the very roots of Shakespeare's art. Richard II shows himself a futile, even villainous, monarch, yet we not only pity him in his fall, we deplore the overthrow of majesty. The witches in *Macbeth*—are they witches merely or demons of supernatural power, masters of destiny? A clownish peasant brings the mortal asp to Egypt's Queen, and his 'I wish you joy o' th' worm' is sharply juxtaposed with Cleopatra's 'I have immortal longings in me'.

The quality that was Shakespeare's is revealed

when we contrast him with his younger and elder contemporaries Marlowe and Jonson. When Marlowe brought his *Tamburlaine* to the stage he prefaced it with words bold, self-confident and unsmiling:

> From jigging veins of rhyming mother-wits
> And such conceits as clownage keeps in pay
> We'll lead you to the stately tent of war,
> Where you shall hear the Sythian Tamburlaine
> Threatening the world with high-astounding terms . . .

And Jonson's prologue to *Every Man in His Humour* was equally bold, contemptuous, unsmiling and self-confident: he prays his audience

> will be pleased to see
> One such today, as other plays should be;
> Where neither chorus wafts you o'er the seas;
> Nor creaking throne comes down, the boys to please;
> Nor nimble squib is seen, to make afeard
> The gentlewomen; nor rolled bullet heard
> To say, it thunders . . .
> But deeds and language such as men do use;
> And persons such as comedy would choose
> When she would show an image of the times.

Not for Shakespeare such words as these. When he, too, prefaced a play, *Henry V*, his lines lack all bravado: he is almost apologetic:

> But pardon, gentles all,
> The flat unraised spirits that have dared
> On this unworthy scaffold to bring forth
> So great an object.

He and his actors are but 'ciphers to this great accompt' and it is the 'imaginary forces' of the auditory that alone have virtue. His common sense teaches him that even his strength, of which he must have been conscious, is a limited and petty thing when set against the infinity of the universe and the vastness of nature.

There is yet a second aspect of this quality. We turn, let us say, to Wordsworth and find the lines:

> To me the meanest flower that blows can give
> Thoughts that do often lie too deep for tears.

Now, the sentiment or mood expressed here moves so far beyond ordinary experience that only after the passage of more than a century have we come to realize that within the direct simplicity of the sentence is enshrined a deeply experienced reality. Even such a realization, however, hardly persuades the majority of readers to do more than appreciate Wordsworth's sincerity; the experience itself remains something belonging to the poet and does not become reproduced in the reader's mind. Shakespeare has his difficulties, but they are not of this sort. His experiences seem to lie within the range of common vision: although many of his characters may be extraordinary, their thoughts and passions are such that they easily come within the range of ordinary life. Of the mystic's vision we find but little in his writing. His power derives rather from the penetrating expression of what we all have felt or feel we could feel than from the enunciation of strange and esoteric fancies.

Nature, the second eighteenth-century concept, may be viewed, of course, in diverse ways. In the widest significance, the impression is given us that Shakespeare *is* nature. There is in him a peculiar simplicity that moves hand in hand with complexity: there is a vastness of conception that seems to make his plays not the work of one man but of all men.

It is not only that Shakespeare, the author, rarely intrudes as a doctrinaire philosopher: always he tries to be basically fair, with Nature's own implacable and unprejudiced fairness, and if at times he fails, the resultant weakness becomes immediately apparent. From his works arises an impression of quiet strength, not placid or won without turmoil of spirit, but essentially serene and all-embracing. In that asp scene of *Antony and Cleopatra*, it is more than the contrast between the deadly insect and the clownish messenger that is important: the scene reveals to us that never for a moment, in all this mighty tragedy which has brought to ruin a very demigod and which has racked the worlds of Egypt and of Rome, has Shakespeare lost sight of those whose lives lie far outside the orbit of Antony and his mistress. Shakespeare may revel in the heroic but the humble is ever in his mind. If there is cruelty in him, it is Nature's cruelty, and his compassion is Nature's, too.

Often has attention been drawn to the peculiarly sensitive picture of poor Wat, the hare, in *Venus and Adonis*, but this is merely one example of a quality everywhere apparent in his works. He seems able, not merely to appreciate, but to enter into the innermost lives of the lowliest creatures. The snail,

> whose tender horns being hit,
> Shrinks backward in his shelly cave with pain.

is for him a sentient being, with which he immediately identifies himself. He knows, as if from his own experience, that

> the poor beetle, that we tread upon,
> In corporal sufferance finds a pang as great
> As when a giant dies.

The term Nature, when associated with such as Shakespeare, may, and does, mean other things. It implies an ordering power that, as it were, explains the natural world, finds patterns amid the apparent confusion of living things, draws forth (rather than imposes) a design. It implies the strength to create in terms equal to that of Nature herself. One of the earliest critical comments on Shakespeare, contributed by Addison to *The Spectator*, makes the observation that the dramatist has introduced into his works supernatural creatures, such as the fairies of *A Midsummer Night's Dream*, Ariel and Caliban in *The Tempest*, which exist nowhere in the world; these, however, he has so created that we feel, if they actually had had a real existence, they could have acted, thought and spoken in no other manner. It implies, too, a contemplation of the world and its creatures, not from a single limited point of view, but with a penetrating vision which embraces all things. Man, the subject of the plays, is an animal living in natural surroundings. He can be looked on as a creature in association with these surroundings; he can be looked on as a social animal in association with his human fellows; and he can be looked on as an individual associated with something vaster, with the entire universe, with the infinite eternal, with God. These three planes of perception, in Shakespeare's mature dramas, are focused into one dazzling beam of intuition. The story of Macbeth is that of an ambitious individual who murders his king in order to gain a crown and who finds that the wages of sin is death: in addition to that it is a political study, wherein an entire nation is racked and torn because of Macbeth's crime; and, beyond even this, we gain the impression that the evil let out by Macbeth has penetrated to the farthest reaches of the universe:

*Old Man.*                         'Tis unnatural,
  Even like the deed that's done.  On Tuesday last,
  A falcon, towering in her pride of place,
  Was by a mousing owl hawk'd at and kill'd.
*Ross.* And Duncan's horses—a thing most strange and
      certain—
  Beauteous and swift, the minions of their race,
  Turn'd wild in nature, broke their stalls, flung out,
  Contending 'gainst obedience, as they would make
  War with mankind.
*Old Man.*      'Tis said they eat each other.
*Ross.* They did so, to the amazement of mine eyes
  That look'd upon't.

The planes are not held distinct, with emphasis now on one, now on another: they exist as a single unity and the metaphysical is subsumed in the physical.

Above all, however, the word Nature applies to Shakespeare's power in the creation of character. What continually has captured the attention of the critics, as it has seized upon the attention of the spectators, is the dramatist's almost miraculous ability to make his characters seem real, to breathe into them the spirit of life. We know, of course, and the playwright himself knew, that they are not real, that they are not simply faithful delineations of existing forms. Had they been naturalistic representations of such a kind, they would have long since suffered the fate of all mortality and died. As it is, fashioned with a vitality which goes beyond nature's strength, they continue even now to move and have their being. Shakespeare's intuitional and creative power has thus built things greater than nature. Maybe the young Raleigh might have sat for the portrait of Hamlet, but, although we know much of Raleigh's life, no biographical study, however brilliantly written, could give us such an impression of *livingness* as Hamlet does. The actual Raleigh moved on the plane of this earth; Hamlet, cast in idealizing terms, possesses a peculiar double personality—he is at once greater than actual life, existent beyond its confines, and yet more intensely real than the most real of nature's creatures.

Few dramatists, if any, have exhibited a corresponding power. In Shakespeare's plays we get at one and the same time a figure which is characteristic of a whole class of human beings and which has an individual vitality of his own. If Hamlet had been drawn merely as an individual, we should be but mildly interested in him today: he would have been a well-written character, nothing more. The secret of Hamlet's perennial fascination lies in the fact that his creator, with subtle cunning, has revealed here a profoundly common aspect of human nature, so that many men of diverse generations and of many races have fancied they saw their reflections in the mirror of his mind. Shakespeare's prime strength derives from his ability to fuse type and individual, to make, if you will, the individual stand as a type or to make the type seem an individual.

The vitality breathed into these characters is, in his mature works, well-nigh universal. With the central figures, the heroes of the tragedies, let us say, there may be less wonder at his skill, but constantly he exhibits the power to reveal, sometimes by a mere phrase, the living quality in characters of minor significance. It would be foolish to assert that all these characters are intensely conceived; yet we never cease to be surprised by the way in which suddenly lesser men and women step out of their trivial rôles and assume an interest of their own. What sudden light, for example, is mysteriously shed on the drivelling Nathaniel in *Love's Labour's Lost* as we listen to Costard's words:

> There, an't shall please you, a foolish mild man; an honest man, look you, and soon dasht. He is a marvellous good neighbour, faith, and a very good bowler; but, for Alisander,—alas you see how 'tis,— a little o'er-parted.

How vividly Launce's being is revealed to us as he talks to his dog. Launce has, he says, confessed to making the messes of which this cur had been guilty:

> How many masters would do this for his servant? Nay, I'll be sworn, I have sat in the stocks for puddings he hath stolen, otherwise he had been executed; I have stood on the pillory for geese he hath kill'd, otherwise he had suffer'd for't.—Thou think'st not of this now! Nay, I remember the trick you served me when I took my leave of Madam Silvia: did not I bid thee still mark me, and do as I do? when didst thou see me heave up my leg, and make water against a gentlewoman's farthingale? didst thou ever see me do such a trick?

With what extraordinary vigour, in *Measure for Measure*, the drunken Barnardine (a creature, if ever there were one, who is but a cog inserted to make the wheels of the plot go round) becomes a living being. Called to execution, his answer is decisive:

> I will not consent to die this day, that's certain. . . .
> I swear I will not die today for any man's persuasion. . . .
> Not a word: if you have anything to say to me, come
> to my ward; for thence will not I today.

With such minor figures, of course, just a glimpse
is vouchsafed us of a living personality. The lines
give us a clue and set our imaginations aroving: that
is all. With the greater characters, on the other hand,
we reach something different. Their vitality is so
intense that we have every right to regard them as
having independent existence. No doubt there is
justification for the smile that now greets any men-
tion of books like *The Girlhood of Shakespeare's
Heroines*, but are those who smile, those who restrict
their imagination to the actual scenes, any less
absurd? A great painter often creates his effect by
means indirect: he wants the person who looks at his
picture to see a patch of colour, but that precise
colour he will not apply; rather, by presenting its
opposite nearby he excites the imagination to see
what is not there. In exactly similar wise the great
dramatist arouses the imaginative process whereby
what happens to the characters between scene and
scene attains a reality hardly less intense than the
reality of their presence on the stage. Shakespeare
certainly did not conceive these men and women as
existing only as the call-boy summoned them from
the tyring room: rather did he seek to make clear, by
indirect means, his awareness of their actions during
those times when perforce they remained unseen.
From his earliest writings he adopted the trick of
introducing characters in the midst of conversation.

> Therefore give out you are of Epidamnum,
> Lest that your goods too soon be confiscate,

says the First Merchant as he enters the stage with Antipholus of Syracuse in *The Comedy of Errors.* The very first lines of *The Two Gentlemen of Verona* are Valentine's

> Cease to persuade, my loving Proteus—

drawing the fictional action of the play into the orbit of reality.

Still another aspect of this subject demands underlining. This living quality of Shakespeare's characters means that they are created in moulds different from those used by most playwrights. There may be complexity in the persons introduced by others upon the boards, but in general these dramatic characters may be viewed only in one way: although we may continue to observe subtleties and reveal unsuspected delicacies in theatrical planning, the essential features of the playwrights' creations remain constant and undebatable. But what are we to say of Shakespeare's art in this respect? Hamlet for different readers, spectators and actors has assumed entirely variant features; Shylock seems to some a mere villain, for others he has the qualities of tragic greatness; to this man, as we have seen, Isabella's virtue is divine, to that man her virtue is something rancid. The truth seems to be that such a three-dimensional and dynamic quality has been invested by Shakespeare upon these his creations that they share the qualities of actual living persons. In real life the hero of some may by no means be the hero of all, and purity on occasion by some eyes may be viewed as a vice. As a man or a woman turns before us, we may be now repelled and now attracted; and, as fresh actions or words succeed earlier actions or words, we may come to despise the person we had admired or to find pity and even admiration for him we had previously condemned. The same is true of Shakespeare's characters. Only those one-sided critics are wrong who endeavour to impose on his works concepts proper to a two-dimensional and static artistry. Just as for living persons, we are within our rights when we say that Hamlet, Shylock and Isabella seem to us this or that, when on the basis of such an assessment, we pass our own moral judgements upon their actions; if we go further and assert that Shakespeare conceived Hamlet, Shylock or Isabella as precisely this or that, we are both erring and revealing our inability to appreciate the measure of the dramatist's art. What happens in a typical Shakespearian drama is that, although it is governed by a central concept, its characters are many-sided, organically conceived and capable of almost infinite variety in interpretation.

In making this observation, of course, we must again keep on our guard, remembering that these characters have their only being in the words that Shakespeare has provided for them. This means that never for a moment may it be forgotten that he was a poet and that the poetry is integral to the play. Lamb's *Tales from Shakespeare* are pretty things, no doubt, but they bear hardly the slightest relationship to the dramas from which they are taken. The virtue that lies in these works is, in the main, a literary value. No doubt Shakespeare has such craft that a great deal of his force may pass over even into translations, so that his art retains its transmogrified magic where Racine's is dissipated; but fundamentally there persists such identity of character and original lines that divorce between them spells confusion.

The art of creating a fitting word-instrument for his concepts did not come to Shakespeare at once or without toil. His early lyricism only slowly was modelled into the subtle forms habitual to him in the period of his maturity. When that period of his maturity came, however, he was clearly master of a dramatic language richer in range and profounder in implication than that of any playwright who has ever lived.

Essentially the secret of this language is to be found in its dynamic quality and in its extreme sensitivity to the meanings and sounds of words. In non-dramatic poetry, the lines need not be dynamic: indeed, there are many forms of lyrical and philosophic verse where the very essence of the poem demands the suppression of a sense of movement. The verbs may nearly all be static in implication and the cadences may suggest the arresting of time's movement. In drama such methods will not serve; a play is a thing of time's quality and movement is of its very being. If we consider carefully the weaknesses of many later poetic dramas we come to recognize that usually those weaknesses may be traced back to a discrepancy between the action and the word, by the application to the theatre of a style of utterance proper only to lyrical efforts. Listen to any piece of Shakespeare's writing and we realize that, even although a single person may be delivering a soliloquy, our imaginations are set a-moving by the dynamic words employed.

> Tomorrow, and tomorrow, and tomorrow,
> *Creeps* in this petty *pace* from day to day,

To the last syllable of recorded time,
And all our yesterdays have *lighted* fools
The *way* to dusty death. Out, out, brief candle!
Life's but a *walking* shadow; a poor player
That *struts* and *frets* his hour upon the stage . . .

Time is a moving thing here, conducting human
beings, as though it were a link-boy, along the toilsome road towards death. The shadow, that is life,
walks, and the miserable actor struts and frets.
Although Macbeth himself remains motionless on the
boards, these words set all things around him in
restless agitation.

Look where we will, the same quality is apparent.
Even Hamlet's most famous and meditative soliloquy has stress and movement within it: 'the slings
and arrows of outrageous fortune . . . take arms
against a sea of troubles, And by opposing end them
. . . the thousand natural shocks That flesh is heir to
. . . what dreams may come, When we have shuffled
off this mortal coil . . . the whips and scorns of time
. . . who would fardels bear, To grunt and sweat
under a weary life . . . from whose bourn No traveller
returns . . . fly to others that we know not of . . . their
currents turn awry, And lose the name of action'—
the words keep our minds advancing and retreating,
straining and heaving, although the actor who speaks
them may utter his lines without gesture, without
stepping from one fixed position on the stage.

This dynamic quality is enforced both by vast
range in style and by carefully placed emphasis. It
has been said, and with considerable truth, that
Shakespeare's genius as a poet-dramatist is less to
be seen in the terrifying outbursts of *Lear* than in the
tragic simplicity of 'Pray you, undo this button.'

What this statement serves to demonstrate is that
the mature Shakespeare has his material and his
style so under rigorous command that, even when he
is dealing with the terrors of this almost prehistoric
world, he knows when precisely he may move from
the sublime without crashing down into the ridiculous. Still another comment has been made on this
line in *King Lear*. The King's 'Pray you, undo this
button' is followed by a 'Thank you, sir'—and our
minds go back to a similar, yet wholly different, piece
of dialogue in the third act. Contemplating Edgar
and seeing his ragged nakedness as 'the thing itself',
Lear cries 'Off, off, you lendings! Come, unbutton
here.' No doubt in the theatre no spectator could
be conscious of the connexion, yet the theatre is a
strange place, where imaginations are quickened and
where more is appreciated than the intellect will allow
or acknowledge; and some kind of vague memory
may well linger on from the mad scene on the heath
to the last lines of the play. If so, the contrast is revealing: in the first there is a command, the imperious
order of the monarch whose angry spirit has not yet
been subdued; in the other, we are confronting one
who has become chastened by the fire of experience
and whose commands have become requests.

Had this been a solitary instance of stylistic repetition we might have thought the similarity in the two
phrases might be fortuitous: but this is precisely
what we find in all Shakespeare's works again and
again. Shakespeare, as a practising dramatist, early
learned that in the playhouse mere suggestions will,
if carefully placed, by indirection serve to find direction out. Often one hears the objection: 'But these
things are observed only when the plays are

meticulously scanned by a scholar: no *audience* could possibly perceive them.' Shakespeare undoubtedly knew better. He was aware that when Richard II, referring to Bolingbroke, makes the comment:

> How high a pitch his resolution soars!

the Elizabethan spectators, knowing that 'pitch' was the highest flight of a falcon, would catch the allusion to Bolingbroke's ambition, and, catching this, that Richard's later reference to

> the eagle-winged pride
> Of sky-aspiring and ambitious thoughts

would fall unconsciously into place with it. He knew that in *Macbeth* the witches' 'lost and won . . . fair is foul' would combine, like a stereoscopic picture properly viewed, with the later words of Duncan on the Thane of Cawdor—'What he hath lost, noble Macbeth hath won' and with Macbeth's 'So foul and fair a day I have not seen.'

Another thing Shakespeare must have realized. In the theatre the very sound of the lines, apart from their meaning, has potent force. Mellifluous utterance is not enough: indeed, a honey-like sweetness will be apt to pall and cloy. What the stage demands is constant variety and bold emphasis. The result is that Shakespeare's language is full of sharp alliteration in key passages, alliteration so blatant one might certainly have condemned it in non-dramatic verse but, being designed for drama, continually stirring the mind and challenging attention. The witches'

> *F*air is *f*oul and *f*oul is *f*air,
> *H*over through the *f*og and *f*ilthy air

is no exception. Hamlet's 'A little more than kin,

and less than kind!', where sound and sense coincide emphatically, is just such an alliterative jingle as we need at this moment of the Prince's first utterance. Lear's

> Infect her *b*eauty,
> You *f*en-suck'd *f*ogs, drawn by the *p*ow'r*f*ul sun,
> To *f*all and *b*last her *p*ride;

Macbeth's

>           Now o'er the *o*ne half-*w*orld
> Nature seems dead, and *w*icked dreams abuse
> The curtain'd sleep: *W*itchcraft celebrates
> Pale Hecate's offerings; and *w*ither'd murther,
> Alarum'd by his sentinel, the *w*olf,
> *W*hose *h*owl's his *w*atch, thus with his stealthy pace,
> With Tarquin's ravishing strides, towards his design
> Moves like a ghost;

his '*p*etty *p*ace', his '*w*ay to *d*usty *d*eath'—all of these are but diverse manifestations of a general trend. More subtly we find it in the soliloquy that Hamlet utters after listening to the Player's speech. After the reference to Hecuba the actor needs a rising crescendo, and Shakespeare provides it for him:

> What would h*e* do,
> Had h*e* the motive and the cue for passion
> That I have. H*e* would drown the stage with t*e*ars,
> And cl*e*ave the general *e*ar with horrid sp*e*ech;
> Make mad the guilty and appal the fr*e*e,
> Confound the ignorant, and amaze inde*e*d
> The very faculties of *e*yes and *e*ars.

Hamlet's 'kin' and 'kind' illustrates another source of Shakespeare's stylistic strength. Constantly his mind is alert to the diverse meanings and implications of words, and often it is almost impossible to

say with finality that in using a particular word or
phrase Shakespeare meant precisely this or that: we
shall probably be nearer the truth if we imagine that
the word or phrase came to him with all the fullness
of its being. A recent comment on a word used in
*Richard II* may serve as an illustration. The King
is speaking:

> For within the hollow crown
> That rounds the mortal temples of a king
> Keeps Death his court, and there the antic sits,
> Scoffing his state and grinning at his pomp,
> Allowing him a breath, a little scene,
> To monarchize, be fear'd and kill with looks,
> Infusing him with self and vain conceit,
> As if this flesh which walls about our life
> Were brass impregnable, and *humour'd* thus
> Comes at the last and with a little pin
> Bores through his castle wall, and farewell king!

What does 'humour'd' mean here—or, rather, what
may have been in Shakespeare's mind when he
selected it out of his verbal treasury? The dictionaries record it as signifying 'indulged' and 'in a
(specified) humour'. The phrase might, accordingly,
be construed as 'Death having indulged himself', or
'the king having been indulged', or 'while the king
is in this humour'. Any one of these three construc-
tions will serve, but we may indeed believe that
Shakespeare, in the heat of writing, caught the spark
that was this word, creating a phrase in which all the
senses of humouring are revealed.

Although a scrutiny of the early plays demonstrates that he was not entirely the 'artless' dramatist imagined by some critics, we must believe, of

course, that the inner virtues of this verbal magic
came to him untaught. At the same time the qualities of his poetic art correspond to the qualities
exhibited elsewhere in his treatment of characters
and in his handling of dramatic themes. There is in
his work no sign of any doctrinaire theory of composition such as was evident in the writings of some at
least among his contemporaries. His method of
expression, of course, changed with the passing of
the years, but only in his earliest, apprentice plays do
we consciously feel the imposition of 'style' upon the
personalities of his dramatic figures. Elsewhere, we
either accept unconsciously the words that come to
us, or, if we proceed to analyse them, appreciate
the quality that permitted Shakespeare to adapt this
rich poetic utterance of his to stage requirements in
such a way that the reality of life as we know it is not
contrasted with what proceeds on the stage—rather
that what proceeds on the stage seems, for the
moment, a sublimation of the real.

II

If we hold fast to these concepts of Nature and of
Common Sense, and if we never fail to look upon
Shakespeare with double vision, a safe path through
the great expanse of modern criticism may easily be
found. The difficulty is that the majority of the
critics are inclined to adopt a single point of view and
to select from the plays only those scenes or words
which fit their own particular interpretations, ignor-
ing (consciously or unconsciously) others which would
throw a different light on the particular subject in
question. We must, therefore, constantly be on our
guard; but, if we are aware of the danger, the task

should not be hard to discover, in these riches,
material from which a comprehensive vision may
arise.

A rapid survey of some among the most common
modern approaches may be of service here. There is,
for example, the school which goes back to such
romantic criticism as was brilliantly produced by
Coleridge. By these writers Shakespeare's works are
considered as works of art completely divorced from
the age in which they were written, and the interpretation is one which makes no allowance for the conditions amid which he created his dramas. Sharply
opposed is the school of thought which identifies
Shakespeare precisely as an Elizabethan, which seeks
to determine the current thought of his time and
which refuses to allow the poet to move outside of
this orbit. Both these schools have produced critical
comments of deepest value, and yet both, being one-
sided, are wrong. The truth lies somewhere in a
region bordering on both their territories. Of course,
Shakespeare was a denizen of Elizabeth's England
and of course he was to a large extent bound by the
concepts of his age: at the same time, there is justification for the remark recently made by one of the
wisest among modern scholars that, when we scruti-
nize Shakespeare carefully, he assumes shape before
us as one of the least typical of all Elizabethans. In
a sense his greatness derives from the strange magic
through which he found the power to delve beyond
the surface of contemporary habit and opinion,
reaching down to basic human roots timeless in
quality. Had Shakespeare been only an Elizabethan
in the narrow sense of the term, we should hardly
now be prepared to see in his characters recognizable

living figures akin to the men and women of our own generations.

This means that, while on the one hand we must be careful not to construe Shakespeare's plays as though they had been written the day before yesterday, we must equally refuse to submit the Shakespeare of our imagination to the limitations of the common thought of his time. We must allow for a difference in appreciation between the average run of uncritical spectators in his theatre and the poet's own conceptions. There can be little doubt that *The Merchant of Venice* exploited anti-semitic sentiments aroused by the supposed attempt on the part of the Jewish doctor Lopez to murder Queen Elizabeth, but any attempt to confine Shakespeare's vision within this range is futile. It is as absurd to present this play on the stage with Shylock a sympathetic hero as to present it in anti-semitic terms. We cannot read *The Merchant of Venice* aright without seeing Shylock as the villain demanded by the plot and, at the same time, as a man whom Shakespeare conceived in such a light that by his side most of the other citizens of Venice appear but sorry, miserable creatures.

The contrast between these two schools of thought is paralleled by the clash between those who insist that Shakespeare the dramatist is bounded entirely by the confines of the stage and those who aver that his works must be regarded as poems. Our judgement here has to be the same. Of course, Shakespeare was a playwright and of course his creations were designed both for the interpretation of his fellow actors and for the appreciation of his audiences. Beyond this, however, it is hazardous to proceed to other conclusions. If we argue that this poet-dramatist was nothing more than a theatrical entertainer, like the trivial author of any ephemeral drawing-room comedy, we become vulgarly foolish. The drawing-room comedy will probably reveal all its author has to say during the stage delivery of its lines: a later reading of the text will contribute nothing fresh and may well serve merely to demonstrate its poverty of concept and of word. With a great poetic drama, whether ancient or modern, we inhabit a different world, and the suggestion, made by some of the purely 'theatrical' critics, that we have no right to seek for any meaning beyond what may be gained from hearing Shakespeare's lines in the playhouse is patently ridiculous. In our own days, the poetic drama is once more coming into its own; if we name to ourselves no more than two of its distinguished exponents, T. S. Eliot and Christopher Fry, we must realize the truth of this. For many spectators, no doubt, *The Cocktail Party* is nothing but a slightly peculiar drama of chatter and gin; no one would be so sanguine as to believe that three-fourths of the audiences who have flocked to see *The Lady's Not for Burning* and *Venus Observed* gained a true idea of what these plays enshrined; everyone will agree that all three dramas unfold added virtues when they are read. If this is true of Eliot and Fry, and of the audiences they address, what right have we to impose on Shakespeare severer limitations? No doubt *Hamlet* is good 'theatre', no doubt a brilliant actor will, by his own intuition, demonstrate qualities in the tragedy we might miss in the reading, but the fact remains that no actor, however brilliant, can give us the whole of *Hamlet*, just as no reading of the drama, completely divorced from the stage for which

it was written, can aspire to distil its quintessence.
Equally false is the refusal to recognize in a Shakespeare play anything which could not be consciously
appreciated by an audience and to read into his
lines material which would be proper only to a
confessedly metaphysical poem.

Another kind of conflict develops between the
'Bradleyites' and those whose minds are concentrated
upon the conventions of the Elizabethan stage.
Rightly, the 'historical' critics have pointed out that
this stage had certain marked rules and habits
which are utterly at variance with the post-Ibsenian
technique of the picture-frame stage. Shakespeare
and his contemporaries, it is said, were interested in
the individual scene, and consequently their plays
commonly exhibited inconsistencies inimical to the
production of an harmonious work of art. These
critics declare, for example, that Cleopatra cannot be
regarded as one person, as a finely drawn psychological study; she is a thing of shreds and patches
each colourful and attractive, but pieced together
artificially. Now, in one scene, she is the shallow
courtesan, now, in another, she is the noble heroine.
A different kind of mixture appears in Hamlet. In
this figure of the Danish prince, say these critics, is a
hopeless amalgam of characteristics properly belonging to the Hamlet of ancient legend and of characteristics belonging to a person conceived in an alien
spirit. And, they add, it is not only in characteriza-
tion that these weaknesses appear. In the old tale
Ophelia's madness was an integral and necessary
element; in Shakespeare's refashioning of that tale
her part is of no real dramatic significance.

The final results of these reflections is to suggest,

or rather proclaim, that we err in seeking psychological truth in Shakespeare's characters, in endeav-
ouring to find dramatic significance in all the
episodes of a particular play, in neglecting the primitive material which Shakespeare has frequently
ill-combined with material of his own invention, in
seeking for spiritual explanations of physical things.
Cleopatra is not a recognizable 'character' and the
much-debated problem of Hamlet's delay is resolved
by realizing that had there been no delay *Hamlet*
would have been finished at the end of the first act.

There is virtue in thus having our attention called
to the conventions of the Elizabethan stage and to
the basic truth that for Shakespeare's audiences
what mattered most was a gripping story accompanied by rich words. Yet the conclusions reached
are essentially wrong. The fact remains that Shakespeare's characters assume life-like qualities, that
Cleopatra does not seem a patchwork and that
Hamlet's problem appears real to us. It is no doubt
foolish to proceed so far as to imagine events affecting
these characters completely outside the range of the
scenic action, but, as has already been pointed out,
Shakespeare himself has given us clues for the
imaginative creation of conversations and actions not
actually put upon the stage. There is, therefore,
every reason for following the 'Bradleyites'—with
due caution—in seeking to interpret the figures of the
various plays in terms of real life.

Once more, what the 'historical' critics appear to
forget is that all drama, and particularly poetic
drama, is a thing of convention. Within the two or
three hours' traffic of the stage there is no time for
that meticulous delineation of individuals in which

the novelist may indulge. The playwright has to work in flashes of insight and he must do all in his power to make his audience a collaborative fellow-creator. If we refuse to allow our minds to pass back-stage, if we fix our attention solely on the scene shown to us, we shall fail to grasp the full quality of his work. If Hamlet, or even a lesser character such as Horatio, has a presence only when the actor is on the boards, if Hamlet and Horatio cease temporarily to exist in our minds when the time for their *exeunt* comes, then the play in which they appear is reduced to but humble stature. Double vision again is demanded, so that we can appreciate how Shakespeare, out of the limitations of dramatic art in general and out of the particular limitations of the Elizabethan playhouse, has wrought his magic and summoned forth the semblance of a life more vivid than reality.

Another thing these critics forget is that the poetic medium which Shakespeare employed possessed in itself a power both co-ordinating and imaginatively stimulative. A great poem cannot be interpreted through rational and logical processes; the very rhythm of the lines, deviating from the informal measures of prose, testifies to the poet's determination to achieve an effect completely different from that of ordinary speech. By the exercise of logical processes we may go some way towards explaining the nature of the art employed, but this does not mean that the imaginative impression itself is capable of subjection to the reason. One of the essential distinctions between the poetic method and the rational prose method is that in the former apparent contraries may be amalgamated into an emotional unity and that explanatory links, necessary for logic, may be omitted. Were some of Shakespeare's characters set in a prose play and their language stripped of its embellishments, reduced to rational statements, we might well agree that inconsistency ruled; but these characters exist in a poetic world, and the 'historical' critics err precisely because they ignore the existence of this world and base their judgements on what, in effect, are illogically 'logical' interpretations of lines whose very nature denies logic.

The 'historical' critics had their heyday during the twenties and thirties of the present century. Although their influence has by no means waned, the still newer school, occupied with the symbolic interpretation of Shakespeare's works and with the study of poetic imagery, has come to attract a great part of the attention previously devoted to them.

Imagery may be defined as the metaphorical language by means of which a poet secures some of his most intimate effects. The force of Macbeth's famous words when he hears of his wife's death, for example, produce their emotional impression by means of a complex tissue of comparisons. 'Out, out, brief candle!' suggests to our imagination at once the identification of light and life, the triviality of life as Macbeth views it and (since the candle was for the Elizabethans an instrument for measuring time) the rapid and inexorable passing of the hours. For Macbeth existence is naught save a walking shadow, a miserable actor in a trivial part, a tale told by an idiot. Unquestionably, part of the essential appeal of Shakespeare's drama depends on the truly extraordinary fertility of his imagination in conjuring forth evocative comparisons of this kind and of enriching his language generally with metaphorical suggestiveness. There is, therefore, every justification for the several scholars who have explored, and who are still exploring, this field.

At the same time, caution is demanded here no less than in the consideration of other critical approaches. First, we must determine the object of our search. For some critics this object is the penetration of Shakespeare's personality and actual experience by the fixing of attention upon such images as may seem to be drawn from his own contact with his surroundings, unconsciously set down in his plays during the fire of composition. It is true that in the course of these investigations certain peculiar aspects of the poet's mind have been demonstrated, but with such a man as Shakespeare we must be extremely careful. Many poets, indeed most poets, constantly reveal themselves in their works. The centre of their world is their own being; and repeatedly they refer to those objects which have most impinged on their consciousness. Shakespeare's contemporary George Chapman provides an excellent example. Both in his non-dramatic writing and in his tragedies he assumes a didactic attitude; his ideas rather than the personalities of his fictional characters are of prime interest to him. The result is that in his metaphors and similes he continually exposes himself, and with confident assurance we might, by a study of these metaphors and similes alone, frame a portrait of the poet, true to the life.

When we compare Chapman and Shakespeare, however, we recognize immediately that their talents were utterly opposed. Chapman, like Marlowe and Jonson, was invested with the aggressive personality; never for a moment can he forget himself. Shakespeare, on the contrary, so readily imagines himself in the mind and spirit of other men that, chameleon-like, he takes on their colouring. At times he may give us glimpses of his own being, but these glimpses are so rare that any attempt to seek in his images for indications of his own particular interests is likely to prove a futile and perhaps dangerous endeavour.

Most of the more recent writers on imagery have recognized this truth, and have consequently given themselves another objective. Their search has rather aimed to find in the metaphorical language of the plays indications of those deeper concepts which Shakespeare, the creative artist, sought to enshrine in them. They have noted, for example, the 'clothes' image in *Macbeth*, whereby an imaginative picture is produced of a man dressed in ill-fitting garments that do not belong to him, or the 'disease' image in *Hamlet*, whereby a cognate picture is produced of sores battening on healthy tissue, or the 'sun' image in *Richard II*, or the image of 'light and darkness' in *Romeo and Juliet*.

Now, undoubtedly, images of this kind assist materially in creating the peculiar atmospheres of the various plays, and there is no justification for rejecting the meticulous study of their qualities because in the theatre we cannot possibly be conscious of them. Apart from the facts that in the playhouse an audience, because a crowd, is more emotionally alert than any solitary reader can be and that, as a result, many things are unconsciously appreciated which might well be missed in the perusal of a text, the exploration of such images is likely to contribute materially to our appreciation of the way in which Shakespeare's mind conceived his particular story and characters. What many writers have neglected, however, is the effect created not merely by the images but also by directly (and not metaphorically) conceived words and actions. If we study imagery alone, then we shall have virtually nothing to say about the concept of 'gold' in *Timon of Athens*, and yet no one can read or see this play without hearing the word 'gold' echoed and re-echoed like a frenzied cry throughout the entirety of the action. In *Macbeth* it is obvious that the idea of 'sleep' is cardinal to the tragedy—sleep, the restorer of worn-out energies, sleep, the haunt of evil dreams for the conscience-stricken soul, sleep, the lack of which brings despair and yet the presence of which the criminal abhors. The sharpest curse that the witches can utter against the sailor who had angered them is that 'sleep shall neither night nor day hang upon his penthouse lid'; it is a voice crying 'Macbeth hath murdered sleep' which Macbeth hears after the murder; Lady Macbeth is last seen wringing her hands in a sleep-laden trance. Yet of all of this, if we confine our attention to imagery alone, we shall hear little or nothing. What we must do, clearly, is to refuse this narrow path as we must refuse the others, recognizing that the investigation of Shakespeare's imagery can be fruitful only when it is made part of a broad-visioned consideration of all aspects of his work.

The study of imagery has proved a potent force in stimulating the 'new critics' towards the symbolic interpretation of many among the plays; and perhaps the most serious task confronting a modern reader of Shakespeare is to make up his mind concerning the validity, or otherwise, of their views. With one thing most of us may find ourselves in complete agreement. In the works of any great poet there are things timely and there are things timeless. What the 'historical' critics have done is to teach us to listen to Shakespeare's words with Elizabethan ears and minds, but it is right we should be reminded that in these words rest spiritual cadences either unheard, or, if heard, unappreciated, by their original auditors. The poet frequently is prophet as well as expositor, and he may express for later generations more than his own generation could conceive, more even than he himself might consciously realize. The work of those critics, therefore, who have sought to arouse us to an imaginative understanding of partially concealed meaning and of deeper undertones must be recognized to have a value commensurate with that of the scholars who have pictured Elizabethan life for us: indeed, the twin approaches are to be regarded, not as contradictory, but as complementary, the two parts of the double vision.

To say this is easy; not so easy is it to determine where to draw the line, when to judge that some particular critic has been considering too curiously, imposing an alien significance on lines of simple import. We may recognize that in many of Shakespeare's plays elements of the old morality drama have been richly transformed into something profound, that *Macbeth* is a metaphysical essay in evil, that in *King Lear* the worlds of Hooker and of Hobbes clash in horror upon the stage and that no one can read *The Tempest* without feeling that in the writing of it Shakespeare must have conceived of the action as more than a fairy-tale. But what is to be our judgement on the description of *The Winter's Tale* as representing an important moment in the history of Christian civilization, or on the interpretation of the puzzling Third Murderer in *Macbeth* as a personification of Macbeth's own crime? Some of us may agree, but there are many who will refuse to pass so far into the world of the symbolic.

Nor does this question involve merely the making of particular judgements concerning the rightness or wrongness of specific critical interpretations. Much more serious is the fact that the problem is one with ultimate and basic implications. Symbolists and their opponents, for example, will join hands in hailing such plays as *Macbeth* and *The Tempest* as masterpieces. No difficulty arises here concerning evaluation, since each school of critics, although intent on its own reading of these plays, agrees in a final assessment. Turn to *Timon of Athens* and *Henry VIII*, however, and an entirely different issue arises. The former of these has recently been claimed, not by one critic alone, as a profound artistic achievement, a great and thoroughly satisfying drama, and the latter as a majestic epitome of all of Shakespeare's work. Since the consensus both of earlier critical opinion and of theatrical experience has been that *Timon of Athens* is like some block of marble which a master hand, in a frenzy of passion, has fiercely chiselled for a time and left unfinished, and that *Henry VIII*, although an interesting historical pageant, lacks unity of conception, we realize that here a fresh set of values has been introduced and that the cleavage in opinion raises a problem of fundamental principles.

The only safe, and the true, course, in the attempt to reach a decision on such matters, would seem to be to hold firmly to central concepts and to reject the temptation to veer overfar to the left or to the right. We may acknowledge willingly that in *Timon of Athens* is revealed an aspect of Shakespeare the man which usually he kept concealed from us and that in *Henry VIII*, beyond the pageantry, is reflected a lifetime of experience and emotion. Shakespeare, like several other great dramatists, did work with symbols, and his trend towards the symbolic, although definitely enough marked in some of the earlier plays, certainly grew in intensity as he reached the end of his career. We must, therefore, reject the confident assertions made by some among the 'historical' critics to the effect that the dramatist was merely presenting, for the entertainment of his audiences, popular stories without deeper significance. At the same time, we must be careful not to let our fancies stray too far and, particularly, we must avoid the danger consequent upon allowing the excitement of discovery to interfere with our evaluating judgement. *Timon of Athens*, whether considered as a poem or as a play, clearly lacks the serene distinction so masterly displayed in Shakespeare's greater tragedies. In it, for the moment, he lets his habitual and characteristic double vision grow single and precisely because of this he becomes the lesser artist. In effect, *Timon of Athens* is Byronic rather than Shakespearian. Similarly must *Henry VIII* be deemed not to possess the central core of meaning, adroitly focused, which we acclaim in the greater plays. From a study of its scenes we may readily discern in it a deeply experienced concept, but this concept has not organically been incorporated in truly effective dramatic form.

This question of final evaluation is, clearly, the cardinal question in all our study of Shakespeare; and, it would appear, our answer to it should depend on a recognition of the complex and frequently paradoxical quality of the poet's genius. He is a creation of his age, deriving strength from the strength of the age of Elizabeth, and yet he passes in imagination beyond the ordinary reach of his time. He is a dramatist, writing works intended for the stage and therefore to be judged with playhouse requirements in mind, yet the quality of his writings and their continued appeal depends upon his power as a poet. We are concerned here with a man whose observation of life was uniquely vivid, who had the creative strength to translate his observation into terms of the imagination and who found for the world he thus set upon the stage the most fitting of poetic words. Sometimes we hear debate concerning Shakespeare's realism and his 'poetic conventionalism'. Such debate appears useless, because what he did was to build out of his mind characters invested with an illusory, independent vitality and to make them speak with individual voices: the impression we receive is that thus would Hamlet and Othello express themselves if they had been gifted with Shakespeare's own power of utterance. Shakespeare's 'realism', therefore, is part of his poetry, a realism deeper than anything the nineteenth-century theatre reformers could ever achieve.

The magical formula, embracing this organic unity of actions and poetic words, forms the essential basis of all his strength: and from the innate perfection of this artistic creation, expressive of the peculiarly penetrating vision with which the poet-dramatist viewed man and the universe, derives in large part the sense of well-being and permanence we receive in reading or in listening to his greater works. Many years ago the German scholar Tieck, searching for an explanation of Shakespeare's genius, hit on a peculiarly fortunate theological simile. He said that, just as God in relation to human beings is both immanent and transcendent, so the poet is immanent and transcendent in relation to the characters of his imagination. We sense Shakespeare's presence beyond the actions of his plays, a god-like presence often shrouded in a mystery beyond the reach of reason and nevertheless potently appreciated; and at the same time we feel his vitality and strength identified with, and expressing itself through, the individual characters. Our task, as readers, must obviously be to avoid the heresy which stresses immanence alone and the belief which places Shakespeare in a transcendent sphere. The one leads us towards seeing his plays in a purely 'historical' light; the other carries us away into the realms of unsafe conjecture. Only through a combination of the two can we hope to grasp the full quality of his art and preserve the integrity of our evaluating judgements.

# CHAPTER III

# THE YOUNG DRAMATIST AT WORK

WHAT we know of Shakespeare's life agrees perfectly with the portrait which thus takes shape of a man possessing such broad vision that his common sense becomes an epitome of genius, whose imagination, based on a realistic acceptance of the world and its ways, soars far beyond romantic fancies.

Considering the facts that the very concept of biography was one of which the Elizabethans were innocent and that Shakespeare was no political figure likely to leave traces of his actions in State documents, a surprisingly large amount of information concerning him has been preserved. Others among his playwright companions remain mere disembodied wraiths; when and where they were born we have no idea, and sometimes their very passage from this earth remains obscure. With Shakespeare we stand on firmer ground and— although we might have wished for the information which in the present age of journalism abounds for contemporary writers—there is still much on which to found definite conclusions.

I

Some things, of course, are likely ever to remain obscure, and we shall not be led very far if we indulge in conjecture where the ascertainable data are ambiguous or capable of varied interpretation. To make wild guesses about such intimacies of Shakespeare's life as his relations with his wife or about his possible early love-affair with a hypothetical Anne Whateley may be amusing, but hardly of general value. His may have been a 'shot-gun' wedding or it may have been the result of true devotion: we simply cannot tell, and even if we could establish the truth it would be of little service in revealing the quality of the man himself.

A very different thing is the making of inevitable deductions based on unambiguous evidence. Let us take a cardinal example. Three or four positive facts link themselves together—his baptism on April 26, 1564, at Stratford-upon-Avon, his purchase of New Place in his native town in 1597, the application in 1596 (on the part of his father but certainly with the poet's financial support) for a coat of arms, and his death at New Place on April 23, 1616.

What are the inevitable deductions from these facts? Except for born Londoners, no other prominent English poet, whose profession necessitated his settling down for a time in the metropolis, died in the place of his birth: Shakespeare's return to his native town, after making his name in London, is immediately revealing. It testifies not only to the deep impress made on the boy and youth by this Warwickshire market-town and by its surrounding countryside but also to the essential nature of his being. His death in Stratford was not fortuitous, nor his retirement there a sudden thing determined by a realization of failing powers. In 1592 he was still an apprentice playwright, just beginning to become known; in 1597 he was only on the point of achieving mastery of his art, yet already he had made his plans. New Place, the second largest house in Stratford, was to be his home.

You do not buy the second largest house in your native town unless you have amassed a fair competence; and Shakespeare's success in saving up enough money within the course of a few brief years to make a purchase of this kind demonstrates that his manner of life could not have paralleled that of the unfortunate Greenes and Marlowes who roistered and perished miserably in London's Bohemia. Marlowe was murdered, while yet a young man, in a tavern brawl; Kyd was arrested because of his association with Marlowe's disreputable opinions; Greene, dying on a pauper's bed, wrote his last words as *A Groatsworth of Wit Bought with a Million of Repentance*; Lyly was imprisoned for debt, and Lodge haled before the Privy Council; Chapman's complaints about poverty were pitifully continuous, and Jonson nearly lost his ears for misdemeanour. From all of these Shakespeare remained apart. That he had his love-affairs is almost certain; the smoke of such gossip as has come down to us no doubt rises from the fires of passion. That he knew how to drink with his companions is also likely, and the tradition which tells of his end, after a merry meeting with Jonson and Drayton, may well be true. But the fact that he succeeded in amassing a considerable competence and was able to settle down as one of Stratford's most prominent and affluent citizens tells its own story. It testifies to his manner of living, and agrees perfectly with the comments made about him by his friends. 'My gentle Shakespeare', Jonson calls him, and the word 'gentle' is echoed by others; Aubrey heard he was 'honest, and of an open and free nature'—which comes to the same thing.

The word 'gentle' reminds us that still another

deduction may be made. In Elizabethan parlance, the significance of this term combined the familiar modern meaning with that which is preserved in the phrase 'of gentle birth'. Shakespeare had pretensions to gentility. About the same time as New Place was purchased, he was evidently giving support to his father in an application to the Heralds' Office for a coat of arms. When he settled down to retirement in Stratford he wanted, like Shallow, to be 'a gentleman born . . . who writes himself "Armigero" in any bill, warrant, quittance, or obligation, "Armigero" '. Yet these very words in *The Merry Wives of Windsor*, so applicable to himself, suggest that he may have looked upon his own pretensions with a tolerant smile. His was no solemn-faced and aggressive claim to birth and a coat of arms.

Similarly, the allusion to *The Merry Wives of Windsor* emphasizes for us that the course of life thus clearly indicated by these known facts of his life is precisely that which is revealed in his works. Other playwrights brought forward their city plays, filled with the noisy denizens of London streets; even when he turns to pen a comedy of bourgeois manners Shakespeare abandons London and finds refuge in a Windsor which at that time was little more than a village. The only one of his dramas in which we feel the presence of city existence is *Measure for Measure*, and even there the treatment of this existence is far removed from what writers like Chapman and Jonson have to give to us. From a scrutiny of his poems and plays we can remain in not the slightest doubt: Shakespeare was a countryman born and bred, and, although he had to lodge in London in order to earn his living, his imagination turned ever to the woods and the fields. Hardly any poet has presented us with a richer array of flowers than he has done, and, while gardens are not forgotten, it is of the wild flowers he has most to say.

Out of his observation of nature, dominated not so much by devotion as by identification of himself with all living things, and out of books his plays were wrought. Shakespeare, of course, was no learned scholar as Jonson was or as Chapman aspired to be, yet we have to bear in mind that the Elizabethan school training (which it is certain he enjoyed) was a rigorous one, producing more competent Latinists than most universities today, and that in the wonder of his genius he was able to grasp in lightning speed what could be attained only after dull years of work by ordinary minds. From school he brought, like many of his contemporaries better favoured than himself with educational facilities, a love of 'that writer *Ovid* and that writer *Metamorphosis*' and, again like them, he freely sprinkled the pages of his early writings with references to '*Proserpina* and *Jupiter*'. On the foundation of this grammar-school education he built a goodly fabric. We must assume that he possessed that kind of retentive memory which preserves, long after the event, clear mental images of what came through the eye to the brain. No doubt he preferred to use a translation when one was available, but there is every reason for agreeing with a modern scholar who, out of his wisdom, asserts that, even if much of his learning was second-hand, it was not second-rate.

Until recently, there has been a tendency to think of Shakespeare the dramatist carelessly picking up some plot or other from a casually perused volume and hastening to mould it into play form. Now, we are coming more and more to believe that he took far greater pains with his preparatory planning than had hitherto been supposed. Quite clearly, he read much more than Holinshed's *Chronicles* when he was writing the history plays, and even when we approach the romances we catch curious glimpses of extended explorations into source material. Sometimes, we may suppose, the peculiar parallels between the plays and works by others may be due to coincidence, to the intermediary of writings now lost or to that of conversations with friends, but even when allowance has been made for all such possibilities, enough remains to warrant the assumption that he was easily familiar with Latin, French and Italian, that he read widely in these as in English, and that he frequently took the trouble to examine several renderings of a story before he himself sat down to write.

II

We do not know definitely when the young poet came to London or whether, when he did arrive in the metropolis, some amateur play or other was part of the contents of his pack. A few scholars would carry back his initial theatrical endeavours to a period shortly after 1585, when he was only twenty-one years of age. Maybe so, but with the evidence for or against a particular time we need not concern ourselves; all we need to know is that in 1592 Shakespeare was signalled out by the dying Greene as a young writer who thought himself 'the onely Shake-scene in a countrey', 'an absolute *Johannes fac totum*' and 'an upstart Crow, beautified' with the feathers of the 'University Wits', and that certain among his plays obviously belong to this period of his career. The precise dates do not matter for us here, although of course it is obvious that the various attempts now being made to reach back with greater assurance towards a determination of the actual years when they first appeared on the stage are likely to add materially to our imaginative picture of the young dramatist at work.

In approaching these early dramas and in attempting to relate them to Shakespeare's mature writings we need some kind of practical guide, and perhaps such a guide may be found in using the terms 'theatrical' and 'dramatic' in a specialized critical sense. A 'theatrical' play we might define as one which, although eminently fitted for stage presentation, does not reveal characters animated with life. Here the author is clearly looking upon his action from the outside and is manifestly fashioning something artificial. In a 'dramatic' play, we might say, the scenes are infused with a kind of inner spirit and the characters seem to assume the nature of real men and women. The distinction, of course, can never be an exact one, but we certainly recognize that the vast majority of the world's plays belong to the former kind, that they may have a passing vogue and at the same time that they rarely, if ever, possess the power to retain their hold on the theatre; whereas to those in the latter category, infinitely rarer, is conceded the gift of immortality because they have been infused with peculiar vitality. These 'dramatic' plays include within themselves the essential 'theatrical' quality, but the 'theatrical' does not embrace the other.

Using some such standard to assist us, we might

go on to say that for Shakespeare, although from the start his theatrical sense was good, the discovery of the dramatic proved no easy task. While it is impossible to assert that his first essays display the consummate craftsmanship exhibited in his later writings, even these apprentice works are well adapted for the stage and there seems every reason to believe that they immediately won contemporary success—but now they have almost completely lost their virtue. As youthful productions of a genius they have their interest still; but at those times when they are accorded a few special revivals they leave us largely unmoved. Only very occasionally can we catch fleeting glimpses here of those elements which, so richly presented in the later works, we have come to recognize as essential 'Shakespeare'.

His start was made boldly with experiments in those three main types into which the First Folio divides all his plays—tragedy, comedy and history, *Titus Andronicus*, *The Comedy of Errors*, *Henry VI*. Let us be frank, and say that in none of these can we discern signs of any extraordinary vigour. All are bookishly imitative, essentially insincere in that they are the work of a playwright who obviously is not really touched by their actions, who is intent merely upon the writing of something which may have immediate theatrical appeal. Their author is a young man mightily proud of such learning as he has acquired. He is delighted to be able to out-Plautus Plautus in *The Comedy of Errors*, to deal with Roman events in *Titus Andronicus* and to insert tags of Latin and French into his English dialogue. You can almost hear the purr of preening self-esteem when the young writer makes the Earl of Warwick conclude a speech with a '*Mort Dieu!*', when he gives to the Duke of Gloucester the lines,

> What, cardinal, is your priesthood grown peremptory?
> *Tantæne animis cælestibus iræ?*,

when he brings '*La fin couronne les œuvres*' to the lips of Old Clifford, or when he makes Rutland die with the words, '*Di faciant laudis summa sit ista tuæ*', on his lips. His knowledge of the tale of Troy is ostentatiously paraded before us:

> I'll play the orator as well as Nestor,
> Deceive more slily than Ulysses could,
> And, like a Sinon, take another Troy . . .
>        And thus he goes,
> As did the youthful Paris once to Greece,
> With hope to find the like event in love,
> But prosper better than the Trojan did.

It is all a parade of learning.

In none of these plays is there apparent a sense of measure. The playwright thinks that the more he says the greater will be his effect. Plautus' twins are doubled in *The Comedy of Errors*, horror is heaped on dismal horror in *Titus Andronicus*, the action of *Henry VI* is spun out into three full-length dramas. In his dialogue the author does not know where to stop, how to make a trenchant half-dozen lines do the work of fifty. Look at the Queen's long speech beginning 'Be woe for me, more wretched than he is' in the second part of *Henry VI*: its effect is lost in a mass of verbiage. And the verbiage is somewhat monotonous. The characters—save for those whose voices sound prose measures—speak alike; the blank verse is competent, but it has little variety and never soars, like Marlowe's, to an eagle's pitch. In drama characters are created by means of speech, and this lack of variety means that not a single one of the figures in these dramas comes alive. Under the surface we may feel the groping hands of life, but their actions are futile, vainly they slip back into nothingness. We see the nobles in *Henry VI*, the villains and their victims in *Titus Andronicus*, the two Antipholuses in *The Comedy of Errors* as theatrically conceived persons; never for a moment are we tempted to regard them as having an independent vitality of their own.

The knowledge that these plays are by Shakespeare, however, makes us pause for a moment before dismissing them. What did Shakespeare learn in their writing, we ask; and are there, beyond the evident theatrical surface, at least tiny indications of an inner dramatic spirit?

For *Titus Andronicus* little may be said. In its scenes there is barely apparent a glimmering of Shakespeare's tragic sense: it bears little more relationship to *Hamlet* than Shelley's adolescent and indiscreet *Zastrozzi* does to *Epipsychidion*. The playwright is revelling here in imagined horrors in which he cannot believe, and, if he achieves anything, it is no more than the provision of lines which no doubt thrilled Elizabethan audiences but which must leave other audiences indifferent or amused:

> Ah, why should wrath be mute, and fury dumb?
> I am no baby, I, that with base prayers
> I should repent the evils I have done.
> Ten thousand worse than ever yet I did
> Would I perform, if I might have my will:
> If one good deed in all my life I did,
> I do repent it from my very soul.

At first glance, we might perhaps be tempted to pass *The Comedy of Errors* by with only a slightly more indulgent comment. Built upon the improbability that twin masters and twin servants find themselves in the same city without being aware of their counterparts' presence, this is merely a farce, and, we might say, it can have no direct bearing on the later comedies. And then, in passing by, we suddenly stop. The very first words of this boisterous play of absurd errors contain the phrase, 'the doom of death'—a truly extraordinary opening for a farce, surely. That first scene, in which the wretched Ægeon narrates his sad life's story and is led off to a 'lifeless end', is wholly serious, and, while maybe the mood it evokes does not remain consciously with us throughout the laughable blunderings of the ensuing action, that serious mood unconsciously colours our attitude towards them. We expect an ordinary farce to remain always within the region of the artificially absurd; *The Comedy of Errors*, by emphasizing death in its opening and by completing the frame of reference with the discovery of the long-lost Æmilia, almost, but not quite, cheats us into regarding the play's characters as real. Not overmuch distinction is to be found between Antipholus of Ephesus and Antipholus of Syracuse, but what little distinction exists becomes enlarged in our minds; one Dromio seems a trifle more impertinently witty than he really is and his companion a trifle more foolish; we sympathize somewhat more than we otherwise should with the shrewish Adriana and her sensible sister; the tinge of the romantic-real, if but for a moment, transforms even the Courtesan—

> a wench of excellent discourse,
> Pretty and witty; wild and yet, too, gentle.

Where *Titus Andronicus* offers us practically nothing, *The Comedy of Errors*, shallow and gritty as it is, has a finger pointing to the future.

*Henry VI* presents a peculiar problem. The probability is that the second and third parts came first, conceived as a two-part drama dealing with 'the contention betwixt the two famous houses of York and Lancaster'—the title, indeed, given to it in the early corrupt quarto. The weaknesses of this two-part drama are patently obvious. You cannot write a really good play on the contention of two houses, however famous, unless you provide a focus in character—and character of the focusing kind is here lamentably absent. Henry VI himself is too weak and ineffective to capture our interest, and the battling nobles enter and *exeunt* in such kaleido scopic variety that they confuse rather than co-ordinate. In places the language exhibits a pleasing, and even a forceful, quality, but for the most part there is little to distinguish one speaker from another and there is a rather distressing tendency towards a didactic rhetoric which never rings with conviction. The theatrical figures philosophize on this and that, but their words are empty.

As with *The Comedy of Errors*, however, this two-part 'Contention' play summons our attention. The political theme may not be so clearly expressed as in the later histories, and at times one may think that Shakespeare is more potently animated by the medieval concept of Fortune than by the concept which inspires the others, yet it is evident that the

6

dramatist is at least groping towards a central purpose. In the very midst of the second part of the drama (*Henry VI, Part 3*), we get two scenes which have a kind of symbolic flavour. First comes Henry's reflective soliloquy in which he dreamingly imagines the contented life of the 'homely swain'. 'O God', he cries,

> methinks it were a happy life,
> To be no better than a homely swain;
> To sit upon a hill, as I do now,
> To carve out dials quaintly, point by point,
> Thereby to see the minutes how they run,
> How many makes the hour full complete;
> How many hours brings about the day;
> How many days will finish up the year;
> How many years a mortal man may live . . .
> the shepherd's homely curds,
> His cold thin drink out of his leather bottle,
> His wonted sleep under a fresh tree's shade,
> All which secure and sweetly he enjoys,
> Is far beyond a prince's delicates,
> His viands sparkling in a golden cup,
> His body couched in a curious bed,
> When care, mistrust, and treason waits on him.

Immediately after this imaginative picture of private content, enters 'a Son that has killed his father' in the civil war in which the king is involved, followed by 'a Father that has killed his son'; the scene has not advanced the plot but it has thrown radiance on Shakespeare's concept of his theme. With this scene, too, must be taken the following action, wherein two Keepers take Henry prisoner:

*Second Keeper:* Say, what art thou that talk'st of kings
    and queens?

*Henry:* More than I seem, and less than I was born to:
    A man at least, for less I should not be:
    And men may talk of kings, and why not I?

*Second Keeper:* Ay, but thou talk'st as if thou wert a king.

*Henry:* Why, so I am, in mind, and that's enough.

*Second Keeper:* But if thou be a king, where is thy crown?

*Henry:* My crown is in my heart, not on my head;
    Not deck'd with diamonds and Indian stones,
    Nor to be seen. My crown is call'd content—
    A crown it is that seldom kings enjoy.

*Second Keeper:* Well, if you be a king crown'd with
    content,
    Your crown content and you must be contented
    To go along with us; for, as we think,
    You are the king King Edward hath depos'd;
    And we his subjects, sworn in all allegiance,
    Will apprehend you as his enemy.

*Henry:* But did you never swear, and break an oath?

*Second Keeper:* No, never such an oath; nor will not now.

*Henry:* Where did you dwell when I was King of England?

*Second Keeper:* Here in this country where we now
    remain.

*Henry:* I was anointed king at nine months old;
    My father and my grandfather were kings;
    And you were sworn true subjects unto me:
    And tell me, then, have you not broke your oaths?

*First Keeper:* No;
    For we were subjects but while you were king.

*Henry:* Why, am I dead? Do I not breathe a man?
    Ah, simple men, you know not what you swear.
    Look, as I blow this feather from my face
    And as the air blows it to me again,
    Obeying with my wind when I do blow
    And yielding to another when it blows,
    Commanded always by the greater gust—

> Such is the lightness of you common men.
> But do not break your oaths; for of that sin
> My mild entreaty shall not make you guilty.
> Go where you will, the King shall be commanded;
> And be you kings. Command, and I'll obey.

The 'contention' is one which affects the whole community and vaguely we seem to be feeling our way towards the vision which makes England a kind of invisible hero existing beyond and yet embracing the ambitiously striving persons on the stage.

In these two parts of *Henry VI* there is little subtlety. The actions and the characters generally admit of but one interpretation, except where, as with Richard of Gloucester, a single person has, through inept dramaturgy, been made into two. Richard appears first as an ordinary brave, if bloodthirsty, kinsman of Edward IV; suddenly and unexpectedly he is transformed into a self-asserting villain determined to 'set the murderous Machiavel to school'. The difference between the 'theatrical' and the 'dramatic' presentation of character is here excellently exhibited. Many characters drawn by Shakespeare in his later works show varying facets of their natures in diverse scenes, but there the whole personality is not lost sight of. Richard, in these two parts of *Henry VI*, possesses no real personality whatsoever; he is simply a theatrical figure about whom Shakespeare has changed his mind.

### III

For all these plays attempts have been, and still are being made, to argue that the quarto or folio texts are merely Shakespeare's revisions of earlier originals. When an editor finds discrepancies in fact between one scene and another or between two separate passages of blank verse in the play he is studying, he is often apt to fall back upon what seems to be the easiest explanation—that Shakespeare's drama has retained discordant elements from the work of another. This tendency, however, may require a check. The only apparently likely example we have of such procedure on Shakespeare's part is *King John*, and a comparison between this drama and the two-part play on which it was based shows a strangely faithful following of the plot, scene by scene, with hardly a single one of the original's lines transferred to the later text. For *Titus Andronicus*, *The Comedy of Errors* and the latter parts of *Henry VI* there seems no compelling necessity to suppose they were other than Shakespeare's own creations.

Yet Shakespeare, and not only in *King John*, does seem occasionally to have based his work on the plays of others, and there is some reason for believing that he may have employed this method for his next essays in comedy and in history. Before 1589 there existed a shrew-taming play; this is certain. Although it is not equally certain, the strong probability seems now to be established that in an early quarto entitled *The Taming of a Shrew* we have a mangled version of this early play, which Shakespeare refashioned as *The Taming of the Shrew*—although, of course, we cannot be sure that he may not have been the original author merely expanding and refurbishing his own youthful work. The history of the piece, however, does not really matter:

what is important is that here we have at last a
play with vitality sufficient to have kept it a popular
element in the theatre's repertory.

At first we might feel inclined to dismiss the
success-yielding vitality of *The Taming of the Shrew*
as due simply to its farcical situations. But is this
play simply a farce? True, many actors and pro-
ducers, regarding it as such, have overloaded its
action with the impossibly absurd; yet the more we
consider its inner quality, the more it must take
shape in our minds as a genuine essay in the comic—
primitive comedy perhaps, but comedy nevertheless.
Its plot is not based, as farcical plots commonly are,
on something entirely inconceivable in real life, and
in the characters of Katharine and Petruchio we
begin to see the dramatic peering beyond the mask of
the theatrical. In shifting his scene to Italy, and in
borrowing a subsidiary episode from Ariosto's
*Gli Suppositi*, Shakespeare has mellowed and softened
the hard, crude lines of the taming plot. Petruchio is
not just a hulking brute: he is a gentleman, if an
eccentric one, the first rude outline of a character
which, maybe because it was the antithesis of his
own personality, evidently attracted the young
Shakespeare. And Katharine is similarly the first of
Shakespeare's essays in the dramatic exploitation of
being and seeming. She thinks she is so clever, the
disdain she feels towards her milder sister is so
assured, that she cannot see either the harm she
does to herself or even vaguely comprehend the
portrait she presents to others. She is, in fact, not a
curst shrew by nature, she is merely a shrew by
affectation. This is a comic, not a farcical, situation,
and it permits the dramatist to suggest an inner

change, not in character, but in attitude. When Katharine declares:

> Then, God be blest, it is the blessed sun—

and adds, immediately:

> But sun it is not, when you say it is not;
> And the moon changes even as your mind.
> What you will have it named, even that it is;
> And so it shall be still for Katharine—

she is not a wife cowed by a brutal husband; there is a twinkle in her eyes and a ripple in her voice; she has become, truly, in Vincentio's words, 'my merry mistress'. And her final lines, although sometimes in modern productions they are falsely spoken as though ironically conceived, well up seriously from a new-found happiness.

Shakespeare's other adaptation was not so successful, although its sequel remains among his better-known dramas. Having completed his two-part play of *Henry VI*, he seems to have turned to an episodic chronicle of the early part of that king's reign and to have planned for himself a continuation of the story—making thus what modern scholars have recognized as a tetralogy. The resultant first part of *Henry VI* cannot be accounted a good play, although it contains some good scenes. Its focus is lost in the diversity of action, and, despite the fact that an attempt is made at the very beginning to stress the theme of faction and civil strife, our interest wanders and we rise from its perusal with no clear vision.

A completely variant impression is created on us when we turn to view the sequel to *Henry VI*, the story of the Machiavellian villain, *Richard III*. Here a different dramatic structure is employed, with the focus all on one outstanding figure. This meant that the dramatist could now escape from what may be called the rather deadening anonymity associated with so much of the dialogue in the earlier plays. The contrast is clear even when we look merely at the opening lines of the two plays. The first part of *Henry VI* starts with Bedford's lament over the dead Henry V:

> Hung be the heavens with black, yield day to night!
> Comets, importing change of times and states,
> Brandish your crystal tresses in the sky.

The initial speech in *Richard III* sounds not dissimilarly:

> Now is the winter of our discontent
> Made glorious summer by this sun of York;
> And all the clouds that lour'd upon our house
> In the deep bosom of the ocean buried.

But between these two speeches lies an enormous gulf. The former might have been uttered by anyone; it is depersonalized; the latter belongs wholly to the one man, Richard.

This Richard patently dominates the entire action, but as yet Shakespeare has not the power to reach beyond the theatrical in the presentation of his character. While this is a marvellous acting part, as numerous actors have found, we never for a moment can consider Richard a living person. He bears the same relationship to a Hamlet or a Macbeth as a caricature does to a fine portrait. He is a mask, not a man. At the same time, it must be

acknowledged that the mask is masterly fashioned.
In Aaron the Moor Shakespeare had drawn a detest-
able villain whose sole claim to sympathy was his
love for his black child; in Richard he creates a being
for whose evil there can be no approval yet who
captures our admiration. The sardonically gay assurance of this self-seeking Machiavel gives him a
peculiar stature, and his power over others indirectly
is transferred to us. For the securing of his effect
Shakespeare relies—rightly, since he is a dramatist
—both on words and on actions. From his own
wonder springs a hitherto untouched vigour in the
lines and a new boldness in the handling of situation.
That famous scene of Anne's wooing has a skill which
adumbrates the still more famous scene of Othello's
deception. Richard's following soliloquy:

> Was ever woman in this humour woo'd?
> Was ever woman in this humour won?

ending with the bold

> Shine out, fair sun, till I have bought a glass,
> That I may see my shadow as I pass—

is instinct with a verbal variety and gleeful vigour of
expression for which no parallel can be discovered in
*Henry VI*. And, in spite of the theatricality of the
whole conception, Shakespeare's characteristic poetic
realism is intruding. Buckingham, who has aided
Richard to his throne, shows anxiety to reap his
reward, and thus the dramatist, in his new-found
flush of power, presents the scene:

> *Richard:* As I remember, Henry the Sixth
> Did prophesy that Richmond should be king,
> When Richmond was a little peevish boy.
> A king, perhaps, perhaps,—

*Buckingham:* My lord!

*Richard:* How chance the prophet could not at that time
  Have told me, I being by, that I should kill him?

*Buckingham:* My lord, your promise for the earldom—

*Richard:* Richmond! When last I was at Exeter,
  The mayor in courtesy show'd me the castle,
  And call'd it Rougemont: at which name I started,
  Because a bard of Ireland told me once,
  I should not live long after I saw Richmond.

*Buckingham:* My lord!

*Richard:* Ay, what's o'clock?

*Buckingham:* I am thus bold to put your grace in mind
  Of what you promised me.

*Richard:*                          Well, but what's o'clock?

*Buckingham:* Upon the stroke of ten.

*Richard:*                          Well, let it strike.

*Buckingham:* Why let it strike?

*Richard:* Because that, like a Jack, thou keep'st the
    stroke
  Betwixt thy begging and my meditation.
  I am not in the giving vein today.

For ease and suggestiveness nothing like this can be
found in the earlier plays.

Even although Richard is conceived almost wholly
in theatrical terms, Shakespeare allows himself to
deviate from the presentation of a fixed stock type.
He seems now to have learnt that the unrepentant
villainy of Aaron is, by itself, rather boring, and he
allows himself to introduce at least a suggestion of
variety. After Richard's naïve prayer—

  O Thou, whose captain I account myself,
  Look on my forces with a gracious eye—

the ghosts of his victims appear to him, and his
soliloquy reveals a divided soul. He can still declare

that 'Richard loves Richard; that is, I am I', but his
assurance is shattered; 'and if I die, no soul will pity
me' is a thought new to him. Even before this, more-
over, a change can be seen coming; his reflection
regarding a fresh murder he is planning—

> Uncertain way of gain! But I am in
> So far in blood that sin will pluck on sin—

does not reveal the sin-revelling Richard of the first
scenes, and immediately after his last triumph—the
bending of Queen Elizabeth to his will—he shows that
his erstwhile fixity of purpose is becoming shaken.
Receiving news of Richmond's revolt, he bids
Catesby fly to the Duke of Norfolk:

*Richard:* Fly to the duke. (*To Ratcliff*) Post thou to
    Salisbury:
    When thou comest thither—(*To Catesby*) Dull un-
    mindful villain,
    Why stand'st thou still, and go'st not to the duke?
*Catesby:* First, mighty sovereign, let me know your mind,
    What from your grace I shall deliver to him.
*Richard:* O, true, good Catesby: bid him levy straight
    The greatest strength and power he can make,
    And meet me presently at Salisbury.
*Catesby:* I go.                       (*Exit.*
*Ratcliff:* What is't your highness' pleasure I shall do
    At Salisbury?
*Richard:* Why, what wouldst thou do there before I go?
*Ratcliff:* Your highness told me I should post before.
*Richard:* My mind is changed, sir, my mind is changed.

These subtler modellings of the theatrical mask,
however, cannot conceal the essential fact that it still
is a mask; Richard possesses a playhouse life rather
than a life in the imagination.

IV

Precisely why the reign of King John was selected as the next theme for an historical play cannot be determined: perhaps again the company merely commissioned the dramatist to prepare a new version of the old two-part *Troublesome Raigne of John King of England*; perhaps one might conjecture that Shakespeare's interest in the story was stimulated by the fact that Worcester, so near to his native Stratford, was John's town. Whatever the reason, we are here presented with an extremely valuable example of Shakespeare's dramaturgy.

Situation by situation, fact by fact, the plot of the old play is followed faithfully; Shakespeare here invents practically nothing. Yet *King John* has vigour where *The Troublesome Raigne* smells of mortality. It is easy to see what happened. After his experience in penning *Henry VI*, the dramatist must have realized that a mere scenic narrative is not enough, that admiration for character has to be aroused: at the same time John is, like Henry VI, a strengthless character with whom nothing can be done of the kind exemplified in *Richard III*. What the playwright does is to seize upon some tentative suggestions in the older play and transform the Bastard Faulconbridge into a vividly conceived person. By making this arresting character John's most faithful adherent, not only is the king's spineless nature given a specious virtue but also a central governing concept is infused into the plot.

The important thing to observe here is that the Bastard, a man with qualities not unlike those of Petruchio and gifted, like Richard III, with an infectious humour, stands out as Shakespeare's first truly dramatic character. He has a complexity which makes him seem real; he is a man who in turn displays different facets of his being. At one moment he is a madcap; at another he is a self-seeking climber; at another he is a stalwart English patriot; at another a devotee of opportunism—

> That smooth-faced gentleman, tickling Commodity,
> Commodity, the bias of the world—

at another a plain blunt fellow impatient of affectation; at another a man whose deepest feelings are aroused on finding the dead Arthur:

> I am amazed, methinks, and lose my way
> Among the thorns and dangers of this world.
> How easy dost thou take all England up!

His are the words that might have been spoken by a king more heroic than John; he becomes the mouthpiece of true royalty:

> Be great in act, as you have been in thought;
> Let not the world see fear and sad distrust
> Govern the motion of a kingly eye:
> Be stirring as the time; be fire with fire;
> Threaten the threatener, and outface the brow
> Of bragging horror: so shall inferior eyes,
> That borrow their behaviours from the great,
> Grow great by your example and put on
> The dauntless spirit of resolution.

Fittingly, it is to this impertinently real Petruchio who has come to associate with monarchs that the final message of the play is given:

> This England never did, nor never shall,
> Lie at the proud foot of a conqueror,
> But when it first did help to wound itself.

Now these her princes are come home again,
Come the three corners of the world in arms,
And we shall shock them. Nought shall make us rue,
If England to itself do rest but true.

And, by giving these words to this character who
seems to be not simply an effective stage type but an
actual living being, Shakespeare succeeds, as he had
not succeeded in his earlier histories, in investing his
narrative with a sense of purpose, actuality and
immediacy.

The living quality given to the Bastard coexists
with a new kind of poetic realism in the treatment of
some other characters and with a new sense of
measure. Listen to Clarence's boy speaking in
*Richard III*:

Grandam, we can; for my good uncle Gloucester
Told me the king, provoked by the queen,
Devised impeachments to imprison him:
And when my uncle told me so, he wept,
And hugg'd me in his arm, and kindly kiss'd my cheek;
Bade me rely on him as on my father,
And he would love me dearly as his child.

And then listen to young Arthur's voice:

When your head did but ache,
I knit my handkercher about your brows,
The best I had, a princess wrought it me,
And I did never ask it you again.

That last line, the child's memory, even in this
moment of horror, of the lost, prized handkerchief,
shows the dramatist and not merely the playwright
at work. And the contrast between playwright and

dramatist is apparent, too, in the two scenes wherein
child murder is being contemplated. *Richard III*
shows the newly crowned king soliciting Buckingham
to act the murderer, while the latter can, at first,
hardly dare to credit his evil drift:

*Richard:* Cousin, thou wert not wont to be so dull:
　　Shall I be plain?  I wish the bastards dead;
　　And I would have it suddenly perform'd.
　　What sayest thou? speak suddenly; be brief.
*Buckingham:* Your grace may do your pleasure.
*Richard:* Tut, tut, thou art all ice, thy kindness freezeth:
　　Say, have I thy consent that they shall die?
*Buckingham:* Give me some breath, some little pause, my
　　lord,
　　Before I positively speak herein:
　　I will resolve your grace immediately.

This is theatrically effective, but compare it with
the artistry of the corresponding scene in *King
John*:

*John:* Good Hubert, Hubert, Hubert, throw thine eye
　　On yon young boy: I'll tell thee what, my friend,
　　He is a very serpent in my way;
　　And wheresoe'er this foot of mine doth tread,
　　He lies before me: dost thou understand me?
　　Thou art his keeper.
*Hubert:*　　　　　　　And I'll keep him so
　　That he shall not offend your majesty.
*John:*　　　　　　　　　　　　　Death.
*Hubert:* My lord?
*John:*　　　　　A grave.

The measure of Shakespeare's advance may well be
viewed in these contrasting scenes.

V

During his early years the young poet was experimenting also in non-dramatic forms and was becoming known among the *élite*. The dedicatory epistle to *Venus and Adonis*, printed in 1593, as has frequently been observed, approaches the Earl of Southampton with a distant deference which contrasts markedly with the dedicatory words to the same nobleman in *The Rape of Lucrece*, printed the following year. 'Right Honourable,' says Shakespeare in the former, 'I know not how I shall offend in dedicating my unpolisht lines to your Lordship'; in the latter, 'The love I dedicate to your Lordship is without end.' It is entirely reasonable to suppose that within the interim between his presentation of the first poem and his presentation of the second he had become one of the Earl's familiars.

Neither poem, although both were popular, can be accounted great. Mellifluously though the verses undulate, they never seem to reach anywhere, and the cause of their movement never becomes apparent. Sensual lust is the theme of both, yet both are coldly artificial. Even those lines in *Venus and Adonis* wherein Shakespeare distinguishes between love and lust lose their force when we recall that the speaker, the chilly Adonis, has experienced neither:

> Love comforteth like sunshine after rain,
> But Lust's effect is tempest after sun;
> Love's gentle spring doth always fresh remain,
> Lust's winter comes ere summer half be done;
>> Love surfeits not, Lust like a glutton dies;
>> Love is all truth, Lust full of forged lies.

The basic situations in both poems are not inwardly felt by the poet but are artificially wrought from the outside.

Although *Venus and Adonis* and *The Rape of Lucrece* were no doubt useful experiments in verse composition, and although they provided him with some suggestions of which he was to make later use, the particular verse measure adopted by the poet and the narrative approach could offer him but little of direct service for his development as a dramatist. The sonnets, on the contrary, present us with something of prime importance. Whether or not a true story lies concealed beneath their conventional surface, we immediately recognize that Shakespeare has found the power to make the imaginary fictional or the personal experience seem real in lyric form as in dramatic. The sonnet's shape itself aided him. Structurally, most of these poems fall into four clearly-marked sections, three quatrains and a concluding couplet; each presents an argument in a series of logical parts, leading to an emphatic conclusion. In effect, it might almost be said that the majority are, as it were, detached speeches, directly presented, and, observing this, we may well wonder whether the Elizabethan sonnet vogue did not spring, partly at least, from the current interest in drama.

This relationship between the play and the sonnet becomes evident from the actual appearance of sonnets within the dialogue of some among the early dramas. Berowne thus develops an argument in *Love's Labour's Lost* by means of a regular fourteen-lined stanza, and Romeo and Juliet woo in a sonnet duet. Perhaps we may go even beyond this, and suggest that later, when Shakespeare had long forsaken lyrical dramatic utterance, memory of the sonnet's structure remained in his mind. An example may be taken from one of Hamlet's soliloquies. He has just seen Fortinbras crossing the stage at the head of his army, and begins:

> How all occasions do inform against me
> And spur my dull revenge! What is a man,
> If his chief good and market of his time
> Be but to sleep and feed? A beast, no more.

This might be regarded as a sonnet's opening quatrain. Then follows the familiar content of the second quatrain:

> Sure he that made us with such large discourse,
> Looking before and after, gave us not
> That capability and godlike reason
> To fust in us unus'd.

The third part presents the question:

> Now, whether it be
> Bestial oblivion, or some craven scruple
> Of thinking too precisely on th' event—
> A thought which, quarter'd, hath but one part wisdom
> And ever three parts coward.

And then, finally, the equivalent of the sonnet's clinching couplet:

> I do not know
> Why yet I live to say 'This thing's to do,'
> Sith I have cause, and will, and strength, and means
> To do't.

Clearly, it would be foolish to suggest that this part of Hamlet's speech finds conscious foundation on the non-dramatic verse measure; but what seems likely is that Shakespeare, after his long experience in sonnet writing and after introducing sonnets in plays, occasionally fell into the habit of composing speeches with the sonnet's rhetorical logic.

These 'sugar'd sonnets' of his were passed round in manuscript among his familiar friends, and from their tone it seems likely that several at least of those friends were young aristocratic intellectuals. Within the body of the one hundred and fifty-four lyrics resides ample confirmation of the guess that the young Shakespeare had found his way into the chambers of the *élite*. Even if we refrain from conjecturing that 'Mr. W. H.' is the Earl of Southampton or some other nobleman, we recognize that the quality of these poems owes its being to Shakespeare's conference with the cultured and the courtly. Nor is the recognition of this fact without significance for our appreciation of his growth as a dramatist—particularly as a writer of comedies.

The histories were manifestly composed for production on the public stage and we may assume that, in the main, their audiences were of the ordinary kind; but when we look at the unhappily over-meagre records relating to the stage history of the comedies, and when we relate these records to the quality of the plays themselves, a certain peculiarity emerges. For comedy after comedy there is suspicion or certainty that originally a private, and not a public, performance was in Shakespeare's mind. *The Comedy of Errors* exhibits uncommon stage directions which point to a style of scenic presentation in general alien to that of the public theatre, and the first record of its performance is at Gray's Inn in 1594; almost everyone believes that *Love's Labour's Lost* was designed for the *élite* and that *A Midsummer Night's Dream* was a courtly marriage piece; for *Twelfth Night* the earliest production noted is in 1602 at the Middle Temple; tradition says that *The Merry Wives of Windsor* was commissioned by Queen Elizabeth herself, and the plot refers to recent events at court, more likely to interest an aristocratic than a popular audience; a court performance of *Measure for Measure* in 1604 may well have been a 'first night'; the most plausible explanation of the *Troilus and Cressida* puzzle is that this strange admixture of satirical comedy and tragedy was planned for presentation at one of the Inns of Court.

Into this picture comes the early *Two Gentlemen of Verona*. Although we know nothing about its *première*, both the story and the atmosphere suggest an appeal to a body of young sophisticates familiar with the Renaissance friendship convention and with courtly debate concerning the rival claims of comrade and mistress. Whether indeed Shakespeare's choice of theme was dictated by his knowledge that these were topics of much interest to the aristocratic intellectuals, the fact remains that in this play, apparently for the first time, he adumbrated two elements which were to take their place among his chief occupations. From the period when he penned *The Two Gentlemen of Verona* what may be called a twin double concept assumes diverse shape in his dramas. The first is the transcending power of love, viewed in all its aspects but tempered by a realization both of love's follies and of its impermanence.

The other is a vivid appreciation of ideals, tempered by a downright common sense which continually impresses upon us the necessity of testing these ideals by experience rather than of allowing the ideals to usurp an alien authority over inescapable actuality. This might be put in another way by saying that in the comedies following *The Two Gentlemen of Verona* there is evident a frank acceptance of nature as opposed alike to man's conventions and to impractical dreamings.

Up to this time his treatment of love had not exhibited the qualities now so richly to be revealed. The contrast of Love and Lust in *Venus and Adonis* lacks conviction; in *Richard III* we can hardly call love the force which makes Anne bow to Richard's will (although the scene does testify to the mysterious power of the passions), and in *The Taming of the Shrew* social convenience rules over affection. *The Two Gentlemen of Verona* introduces us to a different world, first, by demonstrating how passion can overwhelm all other considerations and, secondly, by presenting the woman's point of view. Proteus sins against the code of friendship, yet even the man he wrongs acknowledges the invincible force that compels him to his treachery; that line which has so puzzled and affronted the critics, Valentine's

All that was mine in Silvia I give thee,

spoken when he thinks Proteus truly impassioned by the maid he has been pursuing, is a testimony to love's perplexing and unassailable power. At the same time, in Proteus Shakespeare is careful to reveal not the true force of love, but rather one of its puzzling shadows. He sees clearly that chastity and possession by another may stimulate a passion which otherwise would have remained dormant. In *The Rape of Lucrece*, Tarquin's is a 'false desire' for the chaste wife of Collatine:

> Haply that name of 'chaste' unhappily set
> This bateless edge on his keen appetite.

And in the sonnets, there is both a full realization of the distinction between love and lust—'the expense of spirit in a waste of shame'—and consciousness that the poet's rival (real or fictional) is swayed by extraneous circumstance—'Thou dost love her, because thou know'st I love her.'

This is partly the theme of *The Two Gentlemen of Verona*, but Julia brings in a different element. The first of Shakespeare's maidens to don doublet and hose, she becomes a dramatic rather than a theatrical figure and saves the whole comedy from insipidity. From the first lively conversation when her maid Lucetta praises Proteus—

> I have no other but a woman's reason:
> I think him so because I think him so—

on through her pathetic pursuit of her veering lover she exhibits the inexplicable power of love, introduces the world of reality and consequently makes vital the course of the action in which she appears. Not only so, but her attraction brings others within her orbit of the real. The Host is no important person in the play, but momentarily he becomes a live being when Julia, after the torture of hearing her Proteus make love to Silvia, turns to him:

*Julia:* Host, will you go?

*Host:* By my halidom, I was fast asleep.

*Julia:* Pray you, where lies Sir Proteus?

*Host:* Marry, at my house. Trust me, I think 'tis almost
    day.

*Julia:* Not so; but it hath been the longest night
    That e'er I watched, and the most heaviest.

One further thing may be observed in this comedy:
faintly, yet none the less certainly, Shakespeare
shows, through the medium of Launce and Speed,
his awareness of love's absurdities. Speed's crude,
ironic description of Valentine's behaviour and
Launce's turning of 'a notable lover' into 'a notable
lubber' aptly introduce a common-sense spirit into
this realm of romantic posturing.

In *Love's Labour's Lost* the same course is pursued,
with a subtle difference. Whereas in the other
comedy the friendship convention remains virtually
unbroken, its follies exposed only by implication, in
this the smile of practical experience violently
shatters the serious artificiality of affectation. We
get the impression that the comedy has been penned
partly as a good-humoured skit on youthful absurdities and partly as an exercise in style. Here no
elaborate plot distracts the playwright's attention,
here rather is a great feast of tongues. Just such an
exercise was needed by Shakespeare, and he went
about it in the proper way—by parody. In his
earliest plays he had indulged in imitation, and this
so successfully as to persuade many excellent critics
into imagining that among his lines are lines by
Marlowe, Peele and others. For any young dramatist,
however, parody is better than imitation, since
parody implies at once a refusal to bow completely to

the style of another and an awareness of the deepest
springs from which the original model takes its rise.
Truly effective parody is born, not out of contempt,
but out of love that still retains a measure of balance.
From imitation may come the danger of uniformity,
from practice in parody a young dramatist may learn
the essential secret of his craft, the ability to speak
in many tongues while yet developing his own independent individual form of utterance.

The variety in styles manifest in *Love's Labour's
Lost* should be sufficient in itself to warn us that in
the comedy's concept too there is diversity of vision.
More than once the guess has been made that in
Berowne Shakespeare was presenting an idealized
portrait of himself. Nothing could be farther from
the truth. Berowne shows himself as a variant of the
type that had already appeared in Petruchio and the
Bastard Faulconbridge, outspoken, impatient of
ceremony and tempering idealism with experience.
In his famous address on the influence of ladies' eyes
he is certainly expressing one part of the play's
central and governing idea, but it is only part: in the
end, the rebuke directed towards him is sharper and
his punishment is heavier than those inflicted on his
companions. 'Oft have I heard of you', says
Rosaline,

> Before I saw you; and the world's large tongue
> Proclaims you for a man replete with mocks,
> Full of comparisons and wounding flouts,
> Which you on all estates will execute
> That lie within the mercy of your wit.
> To weed this wormwood from your fruitful brain,
> And therewithal to win me, if you please,
> Without the which I am not to be won,

You shall this twelvemonth term from day to day
Visit the speechless sick and still converse
With groaning wretches; and your task shall be,
With all the fierce endeavour of your wit
To enforce the pained impotent to smile.

His 'gibing spirit', 'begot of loose grace', must be reformed; he is assuredly not to be regarded as the 'hero' of the play, a mouthpiece for the playwright. In his presentation Shakespeare's double vision is clearly at work.

This reference to the sick, combined with the darkness that descends on the laughing lights of the court, startles us even more than the reference to death at the beginning of *The Comedy of Errors*. Shakespeare cannot jest without thinking of sorrow, and his jesting is the deeper for it. He cannot dream of love without hearing the ominous sweep of Time's fell scythe, and his love thereby becomes the more profound.

# CHAPTER IV

# MAN AND SOCIETY

IN the course of these diverse experiments Shakespeare obviously learned much, in dramatic construction, in the ventriloquism demanded of a great playwright and in the magic through which alone theatrical figures may be conjured into vital existence. He was now ready for maturer work; and to aid him in the production of that maturer work he had, in these earlier plays, a potent treasury of situations and words.

That Shakespeare repeats himself everybody knows, but what is perhaps not so commonly realized is that, for the most part, the repetitions seem due, not to lazy carelessness, but to an impelling desire for perfection. In *King John* the Bastard Faulconbridge turns on his companion with a

Your sword is bright, sir; put it up again.

Many years later, Othello confronts those who would arrest him:

Keep up your bright swords, for the dew will rust them.

The first is effective, but both the verbal form of the contemptuous command in *Othello*, and its bearing upon the action, bring what is merely theatrically good to peerless dramatic excellence. Continually we encounter similar things in diverse plays. The first part of *Henry VI*, for example, has a reference to 'antic death': the phrase must have haunted Shakespeare until finally it assumed, in *Richard II*, its chilling skeletal form:

> within the hollow crown
> That rounds the mortal temples of a king
> Keeps Death his court; and there the antic sits,
> Scoffing his state and grinning at his pomp.

The same is true of characters and situations, and of these many remained from the earlier plays in as yet not fully realized shape. As we watch Shakespeare pursuing his later career we seem to see him in a constant process of taking out now one and now another of his artifacts and refashioning them closer to his mind's desire. Even such an obviously unsuccessful drama as *Titus Andronicus* contains dozens of situations and phrases of which the poet was to make use in a diversity of later plays; when we consider the histories and, even more, the comedies, this process of perfectionist revision is patent for all to see.

I

Shakespeare's next plays bear an almost mathematical relationship to what he had already accomplished. A single effort in tragedy, *Romeo and Juliet*, corresponds to *Titus Andronicus*; the tetralogy consisting of *Richard II*, the two parts of *Henry IV* and *Henry V* corresponds to the other historical tetralogy; *The Merry Wives of Windsor*, with its farcical trend, has a connexion with *The Comedy of Errors*; while *A Midsummer Night's Dream*, *As You Like It*, *Twelfth Night* and *Much Ado About Nothing* may be related to *The Taming of the Shrew, The Two Gentle-men of Verona* and *Love's Labour's Lost.*

Even yet Shakespeare clearly was not ready to receive the dark kiss of the tragic spirit. Brilliantly lyrical as is *Romeo and Juliet,* and eminently stage-worthy, it might almost be said that *Titus Androni-cus,* despite its crudity, points more certainly to-wards *Hamlet* and *Othello* than does Verona's love drama. No one can avoid being captured by the passionate swiftness of *Romeo and Juliet,* as Shake-speare so intended us to be captured. The changes he made from his original were all designed to set the lovers' lyrical ecstasy against the ominous cours-ing of Time's inexorable steeds, and, watching the play, we are irresistibly swept onwards. But, when the play is finished, we do not rise from our seats, dazed, baffled and mysteriously enriched, as we do at the conclusion of any of the later tragedies. This is a story of woe, not an intuition of the tragic. The social atmosphere of the play belongs to comedy's domain. In tragedy man stands alone in the terrible presence of his god, and evil seeps on to the earth from the impenetrable and incomprehensible un-known; in comedy man is a social animal and evil is a human thing, born of circumstance and conven-tion. In tragedy our admiration, both in its modern and in its Elizabethan sense, is aroused, and the very titles of the plays, concentrating on the personality of the heroes, indicate the focus of our interest; in comedy, the individual is lost in the crowd, and Shakespeare rightly saw that the question of what title should be given to such a play does not matter. It is all *The Way of the World* here, not the wonder of an individual man, and so *The Comedy of Errors* is a fully adequate heading, or, if one cannot think of anything else, A Midsummer Night's Dream, or Much Ado about Nothing, or All's Well that Ends Well, or What You Will. Although *Romeo and Juliet* ends in death and is named after its principal characters, it might easily have borne a comic conclusion and a comedy's title.

The whole plot of *Romeo and Juliet* lacks the immutable inevitability of tragedy: the lovers' deaths are forced, by the playwright and by chance. Here, indeed, would have been an excellent plot for a comedy, Juliet following Romeo to banishment as her sister Rosalind was so ready to do. Nothing could have prevented her save the fact that her creator was intent at the moment in writing a tragic drama. In the other characters is manifestly obvious the spirit at work. Mercutio, owing his being to Petruchio, Faulconbridge and Berowne, belongs to the Italy that gave us the lighter plays, and the Nurse, naturalistically delineated, inhabits the same world. Maybe for a moment Shakespeare has a deeper glimpse when he creates the fiery Tybalt, but the glimpse is but a fleeting one and evanescent.

No doubt we can weave patterns upon the surface of the drama, saying that the lovers find their true being in the death which enfolds them, that Romeo shows growth in character from the shallow lover of Rosaline to the confronter of Paris, that Juliet, forsaken by her parents and all others, stands in lonely tragic isolation as she empties the contents of the phial—but all these comments, even though they be justified, do not add up to making this a great tragedy. It is a brilliant play, but it lacks full distinction, and, in particular, it lacks the fine organic adjustment between plot and theme, character and environment, spirit and substance, from which tragedy is born.

## II

The lyrical sonnet-like verse of *Romeo and Juliet* becomes more happily allied to content and mood in *A Midsummer Night's Dream*. This, the first of Shakespeare's great comedies, presents itself to us as a kind of amalgam of much that had gone before. The lovers' changing affections give us the situation caused by Proteus' inconstancy; the maze of errors reminds us of the comedy of that name, and even the world of Titania is anticipated there in Dromio's

> O for my heads! I cross me for a sinner.
> This is the fairy land. O spite of spites!
> We talk with goblins, owls and sprites.

For the idea of the burlesque play-within-the-play Shakespeare turns to the masque of the worthies in *Love's Labour's Lost*, and perhaps even *Romeo and Juliet* inspires the choice of the Pyramus and Thisbe theme. It is all a tissue of earlier material, and all magnificently new spun. Within the framework provided by Theseus and Hippolyta are set the four lovers, the artisans and the fairies, all bound together by the theme of errors. Through the forest the lovers blunder their distracted way, the artisans not only rehearse a playlet of errors but themselves are carried into the maze. Oberon in his wisdom tries to set things right and only succeeds in making confusion worse confounded, while for Puck the creating of error is his spirit food.

Here Shakespeare first clearly introduces another of his potent preoccupations—the concept of dream and reality; and with it he first boldly sets forth the contrast between seeming and being. From both, much of the inner quality of his later dramas, both comic and tragic, was to arise; both were to be the very stuff of his double vision, of his common-sense view of life, of his identification with the force of Nature. Appearance and reality interplay in these dramas like two themes in a symphony, rising and falling, changing shape, momentarily coalescing and then, once more separate, producing contrapuntal music. Nothing in this world of Shakespeare's is so simple as at first glance it may appear. Gently the moonlight falls on us, and we think of the moon beloved of lovers; yet for Shakespeare the gentle loving moon is not all. If we hear Hippolyta, dreaming of her marriage to Theseus, saying

> And then the moon, like to a silver bow
> New-bent in heaven, shall behold the night
> Of our solemnities,

we listen also to Theseus' 'chanting faint hymns to the cold fruitless moon' and to Titania's

> Therefore the moon, the governess of floods,
> Pale in her anger, washes all the air,
> That rheumatic diseases do abound.

Like the lovers themselves we can but guess and wonder:

*Demetrius:* These things seem small and indistinguishable,
  Like far-off mountains turned into clouds.
*Hermia:* Methinks I see these things with parted eye,
  When everything seems double. . . .

*Demetrius:*　　　　　　　　　　Are you sure
　　That we are awake? It seems to me
　　That yet we sleep, we dream.

It is almost as though Shakespeare were deliberately invoking in these words the mood with which he wishes to invest us as we listen to his play—and perhaps that is precisely what he is attempting. His epilogue, at least, is consciously designed.

> If we shadows have offended,
> Think but this, and all is mended—
> That you have but slumber'd here,
> While these visions did appear,
> And this weak and idle theme
> No more yielding but a dream.

Yet the theme is not so idle, after all: looked at carefully it clearly shows the maturing Shakespeare at work. Various critics have pointed out that in Theseus we have, as it were, a level-headed commentator on the action, one who is never likely to mistake a bush for a bear. Beyond this, however, we must certainly go. We have just seen Oberon and Titania, and it is precisely these characters whose very existence Theseus would deny; we have just seen young lyric love, uniting with Nature's force, triumph over man-made law, and it is precisely lyric love that Theseus would reject. Besides Theseus there is another level-headed character—Bottom; but Bottom has a fairy's kisses on his lips. Shakespeare's level-headedness, his sublime common sense, cannot be restricted within the ring of Theseus' practicality: it embraces the imagination as well as the ordinary real.

In *A Midsummer Night's Dream* the moon's beams fall mysteriously down on the enchanted forest; the forest in *As You Like It* is bathed in mellow sunlight. Both introduce us to a double world. The wood outside Athens welcomes into its glades fairies and Elizabethan artisans; the Forest of Arden is at once in France, in Warwickshire and in the realm of the fancy. The play is a pastoral, yet it ridicules pastoralism; once more we move delicately among the worlds of human convention, of reality and of the ideal. In one particular respect it marks a considerable dramatic advance. The lovers in *A Midsummer Night's Dream* are lovers and nothing more; Theseus is just an image of practical good sense, Puck simply an imp through whose words and actions the absurdities of men are revealed. 'Lord, what fools these mortals be!' this Puck cries, but in *As You Like It* not only does a human, Touchstone, become the mouthpiece of an almost identical phrase—

as all is mortal in nature, so is all nature in love mortal in folly—

but even Rosalind, herself fathom deep in love, accepts freely Touchstone's frank realism: 'thou speak'st wiser than thou art aware of' is her comment. This means that, instead of contrasts created by the juxtaposition of conflicting characters, the contrasts now come from within. Touchstone is the realist, who enters the world of Arden with the reflection 'the more fool I', who so clearly views the absurdities of love, yet willingly selects his Audrey —'a poor virgin, sir, an ill-favour'd thing, sir, but mine own.' And Rosalind, more truly impassioned than any Hermia or Helena, gives utterance to

8

reflections which trenchantly display her recognition
of love's flimsiness:

> The poor world is almost six thousand years old, and
> in all this time there was not any man died in his own
> person, videlicet, in a love-cause. Troilus had his
> brains dashed out with a Grecian club; yet he did what
> he could to die before, and he is one of the patterns of
> love. Leander, he would have lived many a fair year,
> though Hero had turned nun, if it had not been for a
> hot midsummer night; for, good youth, he went but
> forth to wash him in the Hellespont and being taken
> with the cramp was drowned; and the foolish chroni-
> clers of that age found it was 'Hero of Sestos'. But these
> are all lies: men have died from time to time and worms
> have eaten them, but not for love.

It is a gentle world of contradictions we inhabit
here, and in this world even the eternal contradictions of life and death are included. The play opens
with the villainous plot of an elder brother to murder
Orlando; it ends with a religious conversion which
brings the ambitious and evil usurping Duke 'both
from his enterprise and from the world.' Old Adam
sinks down on Arden's earth, starving from lack of
food; Rosalind nearly loses her Orlando by the attack
of a beast of prey. In tone the melodies vary from
'It was a lover and his lass' to 'Who doth ambition
shun' and

> Blow, blow, thou winter wind,
> Thou art not so unkind
>     As man's ingratitude.

The dark tones of the oboe blend with the flute's
happiness.

Because of this, the character of Jaques (whom some critics have been inclined to deem an intrusive figure) must be recognized as an integral and necessary person in the play. With his emphasis on 'the foul body of th' infected world' he helps to keep us from sentimentalities. His famous account of the seven ages of man, ending on the threshold of the grave, comes pat after the Duke's

> This wide and universal theatre
> Presents more woeful pageants than the scene
> Wherein we play in;

and his epitaph on the slain deer places the relationship between man and nature not so idealistically:

> Thus most invectively he pierceth through
> The body of the country, city, court,
> Yea, and of this our life: swearing that we
> Are mere usurpers, tyrants, and what's worse,
> To fright the animals, and to kill them up,
> In their assign'd and native dwelling-place.

All of this has its part in Shakespeare's complete intuition. Clearly he both loved men and feared them; he saw the virtues of solitariness, yet acknowledged the fact that man is a social animal. If we are to seek for his own features in any one of his imaginary characters, perhaps we should look under the fool Touchstone's mask. 'And how like you the shepherd's life, Master Touchstone?' asks Corin; his reply is immediate:

> Truly, shepherd, in respect of itself, it is a good life; but in respect that it is a shepherd's life, it is naught. In respect that it is solitary, I like it very well; but in

respect that it is private, it is a very vile life. Now, in respect it is in the fields, it pleaseth me well; but in respect it is not in the court, it is tedious.

In *A Midsummer Night's Dream* and *As You Like It* the Italian world adumbrated in *The Taming of the Shrew* and *The Two Gentlemen of Verona* was abandoned for countries of the spirit. Italy, however, is retraversed in *Much Ado About Nothing* and *Twelfth Night,* and in both Shakespeare reaches the summit of his comic achievement.

The former of these two plays combines the typical dark and light by means of two intertwined plots —Claudio-Hero and Benedick-Beatrice—united by a common theme. If in *A Midsummer Night's Dream* the theme is error, here it is deception. Don John and his minions, Claudio and the rest all come within this circle; even Hero, when she is defamed, indulges in a cheat, pretending herself to be dead; and over all, as it were, hovers the ineffable power of Nature, indulging in a final and truly ludicrous deception. While the young gentlemen are smiling at their own cleverness in having brought the sparring Beatrice and Benedick together, Nature smiles because these two, despite their affectation of shrewishness and antipathy, are born for love; she smiles when Benedick, swayed by Beatrice's illogical yet nevertheless true faith in Hero's purity, challenges Claudio to a duel instead of joining in mirth at the old men; she certainly smiles when, despite the irritated amusement meted out by the aristocrats to the blundering Dogberry, Don John's cheat is exposed by an instrumentality most unexpected. All is wrought to a single design, and if any one part is misinterpreted, the fine balance will be lost. We have seen productions wherein Dogberry, absurdly padded out and with the heavy make-up of a circus clown, blusters his part upon the stage, and although we may laugh, in the end we realize that Shakespeare's vision was more delicate than that.

It has recently been well pointed out that in re-shaping his material for *Much Ado about Nothing* Shakespeare has deliberately altered an original lover into a mere wife-seeker. Deliberately he has avoided any love scene between Claudio and Hero, and even the marriage is arranged by proxy. Only if this is appreciated can we escape the error of dismissing Claudio as a cad. He is not conceived as a Romeo who, thoughtlessly accepting belief in his Juliet's inconstancy, inflicts on her a cruel shame; he is a young man proposing to make a convenient match and confronted with an insult to his pride. And equally deliberately Shakespeare, apart from avoiding any of those implications of love at first sight such as he had introduced into other plays, has sought by all means at his command to prevent either Claudio or Hero from stepping out of the theatrical world into the world dramatic. For neither can our deeper feelings be truly aroused. This in itself explains the necessity of having Benedick and Beatrice in the play; their rôle in relation to Claudio is as the rôle of Faulconbridge in relation to King John. Life enters and leaves the stage as these two gay lovers come on and depart, yet even when it does so leave the stage the force of their personalities is such that a semblance of reality still appears to linger, bringing its peculiar virtue to the entire action.

The thought of death in this comedy comes from the supposed demise of Hero, concentrated in the dirge with its deep refrain:

> Help us to sigh and groan,
>   Heavily, heavily;
> Graves, yawn and yield your dead,
> Till death be uttered,
>   Heavily, heavily.

*Twelfth Night* introduces an Olivia, in black weeds, mourning the loss of a brother, and its songs combine the thought of love with the thought of time; beneath these love-ditties runs a deep undercurrent of sadness. 'What's to come is still unsure' joins in melody with 'Hey, ho, the wind and the rain.' Again, there is the same fine balance, which may easily be shattered in production. There have been directors, for example, whose Olivia was a half-witted nincompoop, foolishly and rather artificially lamenting. This cannot have been Shakespeare's intention. For him loyalty is one of the greatest virtues and friendship forgot one of the greatest evils. Maybe Olivia's mourning is carried to unjustifiable extremes, but her rejection of the advances made by the Duke, whom she does not love, is no sign of folly save to the worldly, and, if she becomes devoted to Viola in man's attire, that is merely Nature's sporting with her for a space; in her mind and heart is the yet unseen Sebastian. At the end, it is she who thinks of Malvolio and who extends to him a modicum of sympathy denied by the others—

> Prithee, be content:
> This practice hath most shrewdly pass'd upon thee;
> But, when we know the grounds and authors of it,

Thou shalt be both the plaintiff and the judge
Of thine own cause . . .
Alas, poor fool, how have they baffled thee! . . .
He hath been most notoriously abused.

In a sense Olivia is the true heroine of *Twelfth Night*.

As with Benedick in *Much Ado about Nothing*,
however, Malvolio is the character who immediately
comes to our minds when we think of this play, and
his perhaps is its most fully rounded personality.
Shakespeare sees him whole, living, breathing, and,
this being so, he can at once condemn and prove
compassionate. The last word is Malvolio's: 'I'll be
revenged on the whole pack of you'; but the dramatist is no sentimentalist making of him a theatrically
pathetic figure. His puritanical spirit has been fully
stressed before ever a trick is put upon him; on his
first appearance he has won Olivia's deserved rebuke:

O, you are sick of self-love, Malvolio, and taste with a
distemper'd appetite. To be generous, guiltless and of
free disposition, is to take those things for bird-bolts
that you deem cannon-bullets.

Self-love combined with a puritanical oppression
which would banish cakes and ale shows to Shakespeare's eyes as a foul wen, and his spirit remains
content that 'the whirligig of time brings in his
revenges'.

### III

Although actors, and critics, have sometimes erred
in their treatment of Malvolio, either handling him
over-harshly, as though he were a Sir Giles Over-
reach, or sentimentally sympathizing with him

against his oppressors, the task of maintaining a balanced judgment is not over-difficult, because Shakespeare's own balance is so assured. Yet even Shakespeare, with all his genius, found it hard always to move securely and triumphantly through the complex and subtle mazes of his romantic comedy. In this respect a comparison of *Twelfth Night* and the somewhat earlier *Merchant of Venice* is instructive.

The *Merchant of Venice*, along with *Romeo and Juliet* and *Julius Cæsar*, holds a peculiar position among Shakespeare's works. None of these plays may be recorded among the dramatist's greatest creations, yet their stage careers have been extensive and for varying reasons they form popular school texts for the young. *Romeo and Juliet* achieves its esteem from its lyrical swiftness, *Julius Cæsar* from the simplicity of its language, together with the attraction consequent on its subject, and *The Merchant of Venice* from its fairy-tale plot. Each has distinction, and there is no difficulty in seeing why they have been popular: but such popularity should not blind us into believing them worthy of a place among Shakespeare's greatest achievements.

Where *Much Ado about Nothing* and *Twelfth Night* preserve peerlessly their finely adjusted sense of measure, *The Merchant of Venice* comes near to being broken in half. The main theme, that of Bassanio's wooing of Portia, demands for its complication a villain such as was provided in Don John—an unmotivated stock figure carefully pushed into the background. But the villain here is Shylock. There are critics who argue that for an Elizabethan audience, fed by the mob passions consequent on the Lopez affair, Shylock could have assumed no shape other

than the purely villainous, and, directly or by implication, it is assumed that for Shakespeare he was
nothing else. This, however, seems dangerously to
veer towards reducing the poet to the level of the
lowest common denominator of his time, and certainly it demands careful reflection ere its premises
and conclusions can be accepted.

The real question of interest is, of course, not why
he originally selected the story of Shylock and
Antonio, but what he did with it after it had been
selected. Outwardly, so far as the conduct of the
plot is concerned, Shylock stands forth simply as the
evil force which complicates the action. Further-
more, Shakespeare contrasts the quality of mercy
focused in Portia's richest speech with Shylock's
inveterate determination, by sticking to his bond,
to cause Antonio's death; and, once again, for the
revenges brought about by the whirligig of time the
dramatist has clearly the same approval as he has
when the subject is Malvolio. Yet there is something
queer here, and disturbing. Shakespeare needed, for
the requirements of his plot, simply a villain; what
we get in such speeches as 'Signor Antonio, many a
time and oft' and 'Hath not a Jew eyes?' is a
quality which searingly dazzles us with its penetrating intuition. These are not lines appropriate to
a fairy-tale; these are lines which demonstrate imperiously that, however a hypothetical Elizabethan
audience might have been supposed to have received
the image of Shylock, Shakespeare looked upon him
as a man, and, still more, as a man who has been
deeply wronged. Justification exists here, in the
lines themselves, both for the 'sympathetic' stage
treatment of Shylock and for such interpretations of

the atmosphere of *The Merchant of Venice* as are
implied in St. John Ervine's *The Lady of Belmont*.

This means that the design of *The Merchant of
Venice* presents conflicting lines and colours. Shakespeare tries hard, in the mellow lyricism of the last
act, to recapture the mood shattered when Shylock
stumbles from the stage—

> I pray you, give me leave to go from hence;
> I am not well: send the deed after me,
> And I will sign it—

but even in the moonlight sleeping sweetly on the
eyes of Lorenzo and Jessica we cannot rid our minds
of the candle-lit court-room and the darkness surrounding it. Shakespeare's double vision has here
become two visions, hazardously clashing.

The delicacy and subtlety of touch demanded of
the romantic comedy as a dramatic form is demonstrated, by indirection, in this play: diversely, it is
also demonstrated by the later *All's Well that Ends
Well* and *Measure for Measure*. Perhaps the kindest
thing we can do with the former is to suggest it was
penned by Shakespeare in a time of illness or mental
disturbance, and then to dismiss it from our minds.
Its laughter grates on scrannel-pipes of wretched
straw, its love comes close to lust and its planning is
weak. *Measure for Measure* is entirely different.
While only an abandonment of true values can
explain the endeavour, made by one or two critics,
to elevate it into one of Shakespeare's greatest
dramas, we may readily be prepared to confess that,
although it displays manifest theatrical weaknesses,
it stands out for its implications as one of the playwright's most interesting works.

The trouble with *Measure for Measure* is that it seeks to achieve more than the form of romantic comedy can permit, and that it introduces subject-matter which no dramatic legerdemain can make thoroughly satisfactory. In the more successful romantic comedies we inhabit or are very close to the greenwood, contentedly lying in the kindly embrace of a Nature which, although it admits of danger and of death, appears wisely benign. In *Measure for Measure* we pace the dirty streets of a vice-sodden Vienna and encounter a Nature whose visage has completely altered. The cloven hoof treads down the fairies' footsteps; the foul odour of the stews obliterates the scent of the violet bank. It is as though the Shakespeare who thought he had found in lyric love the secret of happiness, even although he always clearly realized love's follies, had suddenly become aware, not so much that lust is different from love, but rather that the two may hardly be separated. In addition, the thought of justice, vaguely present in most of his earlier plays and rising prominently almost into the central theme of *The Merchant of Venice*, wells up now until it envelops the whole stage in its dark and perplexing folds. The earlier plays had for the most part gaily and happily shown youthful love rebelling against harsh parental command and oppressive law; rebellion and libertinism in these plays are alike merry and innocent. Now, Shakespeare's mind is puzzled by the eternal problem presented by man the individual and by man the social animal, by the conflict between the freedom demanded of the one and the law necessary for the other.

The task of building all of this into a romantic

comedy framework proves too great even for Shake-speare's skill, and the confusion in critical attitudes towards the play must in part be laid firmly at his workshop door. At the same time, the confusion is augmented and partly occasioned by our attempting to regard the actions and the characters from one or another particular and limited point of view. This goes further than a mere clash between the symbolic and historical approaches. We err, of course, equally if we regard the drama from a modern viewpoint, as though it were the work of a Bernard Shaw, and if we take a hypothetical 'Elizabethan' attitude, refusing to permit Shakespeare to conceive and create anything beyond the capabilities of the average of his time; but, more importantly, we err if we fail to see that *Measure for Measure* possesses a quality complex and ambivalent. That it is more than a popular fairy-tale becomes self-evident when we turn to those scenes wherein the passions reach tragic intensity and when we note how, from the Duke's opening speech on the properties of government to Isabella's cry of 'justice, justice, justice, justice' and her final unexpected pleas for Angelo, the whole of the dialogue is shot through with references to law, pardon and mercy. We are compelled to recognize that Shakespeare has a purpose deeper here than the mere telling of a story. At the same time, most of those who have recognized this fact have in their turn been mistaken because of their endeavour to interpret the drama as a thesis play, with praise and blame and judgement portioned out by the author himself. What really happens in *Measure for Measure* is that Shakespeare creates a vision of life, and, al-though there can be no doubt concerning the things he regards as evil and those he considers good, his characters, built in the round and endowed with vitality, are not stock figures to be comfortably docketed with moral tags. Isabella is much more than an image of Purity; she is a pure woman, no doubt, and we should not have wished her to act otherwise than she did—but we certainly might have wished her to speak a trifle differently. About her nunnish form clings something of Malvolio's self-love and sense of superiority; for her, too, cakes and ale are deplorable concessions to the flesh. Shakespeare conceived her so, consciously or else simply because his genius persisted in breathing life into the statues of his creation. We are allowed to take sides, if we will, condemning or praising as we should condemn a real Isabella—but in this process we ought not to permit our lesser minds to bring Shakespeare himself within the narrow orbits of our own moral judgements.

Precisely the same problem arises when we turn to Angelo. In him Shakespeare presents his culminating picture of the man who is gripped in the vice of false love; against ordinary temptations he is armour-proof and intuitively we know that not a single painted idol of a woman could ever have shattered his rigid code of behaviour. Only such a force as Isabella's coldness might have the power to fan the puritanically suppressed embers of his passions into desperate flame. Angelo thus becomes much more than a theatrical type; in one sense he acts ironically as the devil to Isabella's divinity, in another he plays the hypocrite, in another he is a man who sincerely and justifiably abhors the evil monstrosity of Vienna's life and who pitiably fails in his moral task because his idealism lacks awareness of the adjustments which the ideal must ever make to man's essential nature.

The trouble with *Measure for Measure* lies basically in the inescapable fact that the romantic comedy form cannot bear with such vital characters as Isabella and Angelo, nor can it adequately embrace the deeper problems inherent in Shakespeare's treatment of the theme. In order to put before us the full scope of his conception of law—the inner moral law and the legal sanctions of social life—Shakespeare has to contrive a situation which will allow Isabella to kneel a petitioner for the unmasked Angelo, and, if we think only of the conception, we may cheat ourselves into seeing manifold virtues in the dramatist's contriving. On the other hand, we must ever remember that we are dealing here, not with a poem, but with a play, and that on the stage the huddled last act, with its series of turns and counter-turns, its scurried whipping on and off of disguises, seems artificial and forced. Like *The Merchant of Venice*, but in a different way, *Measure for Measure* is a comedy broken in half.

IV

When *Measure for Measure* was written, Shakespeare had already composed his *Hamlet* and was in process of planning his other tragedies; he had also had the experience of exploring, in his second historical tetralogy, some of the basic problems of government which, in intensified and deepened form, occupied his mind in creating the Duke of Vienna, Escalus, Angelo and Isabella.

The beginning of this second historical tetralogy comes with *Richard II*, at once a development of suggestions in *Henry VI* and, dramatically, a counterpart to *Richard III*. Again and again in *Henry VI* we encounter speeches and phrases, and, still more significantly, attitudes, which are echoed more richly in the later play. Henry's soliloquy on the sorrows of kingship, his dreaming of the quiet life, is caught up and deepened in Richard's abnegation of royal pageantry. Even the same tricks of style are repeated in both:

> Thereby to see the minutes how they run,
> How many makes the hour full complete;
> How many hours brings about the day;
> How many days will finish up the year;
> How many years a mortal man may live—

and

> I'll give my jewels for a set of beads,
> My gorgeous palace for an hermitage,
> My gay apparel for an almsman's gown,
> My figured goblets for a dish of wood,
> My sceptre for a palmer's walking-staff,
> My subjects for a pair of carved saints,
> And my large kingdom for a little grave,
> A little, little grave, an obscure grave—

or

> With mine own tears I wash away my balm,
> With mine own hands I give away my crown,
> With mine own tongue deny my sacred state,
> With mine own breath release all duty's rights.

When Richard utters the lines:

> What must the King do now? must he submit?
> The King shall do it: must he be deposed?
> The King shall be contented: must he lose
> The name of King? o' God's name, let it go—

he is obviously echoing, even to the adoption of a particular phrase, Henry's:

> Go where you will, the King shall be commanded,
> And be you Kings; command, and I'll obey.

Identical qualities are to be found in each. 'Good day, my lord,' says Gloucester. 'What, at your book so hard?' Henry answers:

> Ay, my good lord:—my lord, I should say rather;
> 'Tis sin to flatter; 'good' was little better:
> 'Good Gloucester' and 'good devil' were alike,
> And both preposterous; therefore, not 'good lord'.

This agrees with Richard's

> Ay, no; no, ay; for I must nothing be;
> Therefore no, no; for I resign to thee—

and his reply to Bolingbroke's 'name it, fair cousin':

> 'Fair cousin'? I am greater than a king:
> For when I was a king, my flatterers
> Were then but subjects; being now a subject,
> I have a king here to my flatterer.

In *Henry VI*, *King John* and in *Richard II* Shakespeare faced the problem of dealing with central characters essentially weak. The first play allowed its central character to become lost amid the clanking press of armed nobles. For the second, a new dramatic structure was devised, whereby a person closely associated with the ineffective monarch was allowed, indirectly, to provide the King with an interest he would otherwise have lacked. *Richard III* displayed still another plan, in which a single figure, the theatrically conceived villain, dominated all the action. Now, in *Richard II*, Shakespeare, maturing in power, creates a new scene; he follows in a sense the scheme he had adopted in *Richard III* by focusing attention on the central figure, but he deviates from this scheme in two ways—first, by substituting a dramatic, living character for the theatrically conceived, melodramatic villain, and, secondly, by developing a strong contrast and conflict between Richard and Bolingbroke. The result is a drama in which, far more surely than in *Romeo and Juliet*, he begins to point forward towards his tragedies to come. Perhaps Richard is too weak to bear the full weight of tragedy's robes, yet by giving him the qualities of a poet, and by so making us feel that on a seat less exalted than a royal throne he might have achieved greatness, Shakespeare has gone far towards arousing in us that sense of admiration without which the tragic scene cannot exist, and, further, he has suggested the peculiar relationship between character and circumstance on which his tragedies were later to be based.

The craftsmanship exhibited here is superb. Until half-way through the drama Richard's folly, his inadequacy, and even his evil, alone are stressed; he is virtually the accused, standing judgement as the dying Gaunt condemns him in words among the most impassioned to be found anywhere in Shakespeare's works. Then, suddenly, on the King's return

9

from Ireland, the obverse of the picture is presented
to us. Preparation for it has been made by the
devotion to his cause exhibited by York, one of his
accusers, and by the loving despair of the Queen, but
the effect owes its being largely to the skilful use of
dramatic imagery. Throughout the first two acts the
emphasis upon England, and particularly upon
England's soil, has been constant, reaching a cul-
mination in Gaunt's

This blessed plot, this earth, this realm, this England.

The result is that when Richard, returning to meet
threatened rebellion, bends down to the ground—

Dear earth, I do salute thee with my hand,
Though rebels wound thee with their horses' hoofs . . .
So, weeping, smiling, greet I thee, my earth,
And do thee favours with my royal hands—

by the strange alchemy of the imagination a great
surge of sympathy sweeps over the audience. In a
single powerful dramatic moment Shakespeare has
achieved what might have been deemed the impossible.

*Richard II*, of course, is not designed as the later
tragedies are designed; it remains essentially a
chronicle history and its theme is English politics.
Whether Shakespeare originally had the idea of carrying on its action is a moot point; but it is certain that,
when he did so carry it on, the image of Richard's
fate continued to stand as a kind of ominous
symbol for the later generations. In the consideration of its politics, however, we must be careful not
to consider too narrowly. Shakespeare's vision
embraces both the man Richard and the King; it

assumes form as an intuition rather than as an intellectually conceived thought; it includes within itself
both the immediate concrete events, dominated by
human agency, and the invisible powers of Fortune
and Opportunity. We can have no doubt but that
Shakespeare himself looked upon disorder with
keenest apprehension, and consequently we must see
in Carlisle's words an expression of his own most
passionate belief; the deposing of Richard is a deed
'heinous, black, obscene', calculated to bring to
England 'disorder, horror, fear and mutiny'. This
is the warning, and in part it is fulfilled. The shadow
of Richard falls darkly not only upon the usurping
Bolingbroke's spirit but also upon that of his son.
Yet the fulfilment is in part only. Although a grave
crime has been committed and although Bolingbroke, now Henry IV, has put himself by force in
Richard's place, Shakespeare makes it clear in the
Aumerle episode that the duty of all worthy men
belongs to the new crowned monarch. The idealism
of an Aumerle must be qualified by practical considerations; enthusiasm, not tempered by the lessons
of experience, may well cause confusion and disaster
greater than what would otherwise have been. And
there can be no doubt but that the usurper has
qualities better fitting him to wield the royal power
than the legitimate monarch.

Into this picture of political events, concerned with
conflicting personalities and with concrete acts,
enters in the larger concept of Fortune. God's ways
are mysterious, and the wheel of the blind goddess is
continually turning, bringing about events not
directly motivated by human action. Very carefully
Shakespeare gives to his portrait of Bolingbroke a

three-dimensional quality, so that we can never
definitely label him this or that. He is ambitious,
no doubt, yet the dramatist has adroitly suggested in
many scenes that his rising to power derives from a
force beyond himself. When Worcester upbraids him
later (in *Henry IV*) the emphatic verbs stress this:

> But in short space
> It rain'd down fortune showering on your head;
> And such a flood of greatness fell on you,
> What with our help, what with the absent King,
> What with the injuries of a wanton time,
> The seeming sufferances that you had borne,
> And the contrarious winds that held the King
> So long in his unlucky Irish wars
> That all in England did repute him dead:
> And from this swarm of fair advantages
> You took occasion to be quickly woo'd
> To gripe the general sway into your hand.

Bolingbroke no doubt grasped the occasion, but
inscrutable destiny had shaped his course; fortune
showered down upon him and greatness fell from
above upon his shoulders. We may assume Shakespeare is making him speak sincerely when he avers
that in the beginning he 'had no such intent' as to
seize the throne,

> But that necessity so bow'd the state,
> That I and greatness were compell'd to kiss.

In this carrying on of Bolingbroke's story in
*Henry IV*, Shakespeare moves back from the almost
tragic pattern of *Richard II* to the episodical or epic
pattern of *Henry VI*. A vast chasm, however, separ-
ates these plays. Where *Henry VI* drifts confusedly

on and rarely excites our interest in character, the broad canvas of *Henry IV* brings us in the end to realize its subtle and emphatic design. The King himself, his dramatic mission done, is deliberately permitted to become a background figure; although long speeches are given to him and although he plays a prominent part in the action, what may be called his spiritual force is virtually non-existent; his is not the personality of whom we think when we recall the play. Instead, Shakespeare concentrates on the contrasting characters of Prince Hal, Falstaff and Hotspur, and through them he enlarges the whole picture of England. In *Henry VI* all we see is the court, the field of battle and the market-place wherein the mob mills wildly and passionately. Much of our time in *Henry IV* is spent in a tavern; we stand in darkness near Eastcheap; we post to a castle in the north; we listen to a Welsh song on the border country. This happy breed of men, merely a phrase in *Richard II*, becomes a reality on the stage.

Modern scholarship no doubt rightly has stressed the 'morality' element in *Henry IV*, but we should be careful not to allow our interpretation of the play to be too strictly governed by such a concept. The morality play suggests the presentation of stock figures for the purpose of inculcating an idea; what the dramatist appears to be striving to present in *Henry IV* is a series of contrasting characters in life, controlled and governed by the fact that these characters are directly related to the central force, the crown, which holds England's order at its command. From the very beginning, the history plays had displayed acute consciousness of the disturbing problem presented by the double life of a king—his symbolic existence as God's regent and his existence as a man. In Henry VI Shakespeare depicted a good but weak monarch who would willingly have given over the cares of royalty, in Richard III an evil, self-seeking usurper, in Richard II an ineffective lover of pageantry, with thoughts concentrated too much upon himself, and in Henry IV an effective ruler whom yet ambition and opportunity had brought to the throne through strife. None of these rulers, however, had appeared in any but a royal capacity; their companions were nobles of the court and, even although we are made aware, by scenes directly presented or by narration, of the people they ruled, their own contact with these people was not actively presented. Nor were they displayed other than as anointed Kings, or as Kings about to be anointed; Henry VI may refer back to his early days but we are not actually shown him in his process of growth. These men we cannot think of without seeing their crowns upon their heads or at least about to descend upon them. When, therefore, in *Henry IV*, we find a fat, old, greasy knight inquiring 'Now, Hal, what time of day is it, lad?' and discover that the person he addresses is the heir apparent, we realize the deliberate cleavage between the old and the new.

This novel treatment of a prince, however, demands careful practice, and hence Shakespeare is forced to introduce, by means of a convention well established on the Elizabethan stage, a self-revelatory explanation. Those lines, in which the future Henry V declares his intention to permit for a time

the base contagious clouds
To smother up his beauty from the world,

in order that men shall admire him the more when he throws off his 'loose behaviour' have mightily troubled the sentimentalists and have been dismissed by others as Elizabethan convention merely. A true appreciation of their force would seem to demand the adoption of a double, and therefore common-sense, point of view. In Prince Hal Shakespeare, guided by experience, is displaying a not unlikeable, practical man who, although he is not driven by ambition to seize the crown before his time, knows what he has been born to do, and whose realistic attitude is deliberately contrasted with idealistic follies. Falstaff is not so much the vice of the moralities as a representative of a certain kind of idealism—that is to say his whole attitude to life and his judgement of events are determined by the imposition of an idea upon actuality. Into his limited imagination never enters a doubt but that the relations he has had with the prince can continue and expand with the king. He falsely believes that he will be 'fortune's steward' and that the laws of England will be at his commandment. Opposed to his idealism is the idealism of Hotspur, the man for whom the serious affairs of strife are all in all. Both err, because they have no mean, because they judge life by their set idea and not by observant experience, yet both are sympathetically and vitally presented. We recognize Hotspur's living quality in his very first words and we are all on his side as he describes his encounter with the affected, lisping and perfumed young gallant who tells him

> the sovereign'st thing on earth
> Was parmaceti for an inward bruise;

at the same time we realize that his inordinate talk
of honour represents an idealistic obsession which
carries him into the impractical region of the
absurd—

> By heaven, methinks it were an easy leap,
> To pluck bright honour from the pale-faced moon.

It is this idealistic impracticality that produces the
ironic 'out of this nettle, danger, we pluck this
flower, safety', just before the collapse of his rebellion. Falstaff's living quality is even more assured,
and his personal appeal has been such that not a few
critics have tearfully lamented his rejection and
demise. But if Hotspur's honour is falsely idealistic,
so is his rejection of honour; his judgement that
'honour is a mere scutcheon' exhibits an error equal
to Harry Percy's fanatical devotion to the concept.

Hal deliberately is made to come between these
two, as it were including them both. Even after he
has become King he still remembers his earlier
pranks, as he shows in the glove episode of *Henry V*;
and his address to his soldiers before Agincourt is
an expansion of Hotspur's

> You strain too far.
> I rather of his absence make this use:
> It lends a lustre and more great opinion,
> A larger dare to our great enterprise,
> Than if the earl were here.

The difference is that Henry knows when to jest and
when to be serious, and that the words he speaks at
Agincourt spring, not from impractical and self-
centred pride, but from the grim necessities of the
dark moment.

In order that the man Hal can truly become Henry V and fulfil effectively his high offices, both Hotspur and Falstaff must perish. Hotspur falls on the field of battle, since his exaggerated cult of honour allows him no escape save death; Falstaff, who preserves his life by an ignoble trick, is compelled to die in life. As Henry V comes riding in state, his very being irradiated by the awful rite of consecration, there remains nothing for him to do save cast off the one with the other. Any attempt to condone the rejection of Falstaff is based on a premise other than Shakespeare's. Falstaff has been a merry companion for a space, but his values are wrong, even as those of the rebellious Hotspur were wrong.

*Henry V* carries on the story with more didactic content. As prince, Hal had shown himself 'of all humours'; now the country united under him is revealed in the four humours of England, Ireland, Scotland and Wales, and the action proceeds, not so much as a play, but rather as a patriotic pageant. After all the self-centred monarchs, intent on their narrow interests, there arises the man whose qualities fit him truly for the throne. He may not be possessed of those infectiously appealing characteristics which bind Richard II to us, but at last we have presented before us the kind of human being with whom the crown is safe. Exercising peculiar care, Shakespeare deliberately devotes a large part of this pageant to revealing the man beneath the robes and the royal armour. His theme is a vast one, demanding special chorus calls for the summoning forth of the audience's imagination. The dramatist might well have devoted all his scenes to Agincourt and to affairs of state; yet in the end what remains in our minds is the scene which shows us the King moving among the soldiers of his camp and demonstrating his ordinary humanity. In no other play, perhaps, has Shakespeare so clearly demonstrated his practical, realistic attitude towards life, and those readers who are regretful that Henry V is not a more flamboyant or idealistic figure are themselves guilty of the error which Shakespeare seems to strive, here and elsewhere, to exhibit.

# CHAPTER V

# MAN AND THE UNIVERSE

AS SHAKESPEARE came to approach his fortieth year he found himself at last equipped to wrestle successfully with the tragic form. Maturity in experience and mastery of the dramatic art now enabled him to achieve triumphantly what he had several times attempted and failed to subdue.

Tragedy, at least Shakespearian tragedy, is a complex of conflicting elements wrought into unity. It stands in awe before the wonder in man, and it flinches before the thought of man's littleness—

> What a piece of work is a man! how noble in reason! how infinite in faculties! in form and moving how express and admirable! in action how like an angel! in apprehension how like a god! the beauty of the world! the paragon of animals! And yet to me what is this quintessence of dust?

It wells up from a deep awareness of evil, yet it never forsakes belief in the eternal good. It takes the universe as its theme, and yet is bound to the men and women set moving upon its stage. Its pity is profound, and yet it is remorseless. It sees that a man is responsible for his own fate, and yet it acknowledges the implacable will of the gods. It cannot take shape unless there exists behind the action a great love for certain human beings, and yet in its most passionate moments its spirit is dominated by fear of humanity. It embraces life, and yet it flies to death like a lover.

Let one of these elements be overstressed, and tragedy comes crashing down in monumental ruin. Even Shakespeare, at the highest pitch of his power, was forced to strain his imagination and his art to the uttermost before the balance could be kept in delicate and subtle trembling.

I

His approach to the tragic realm was made through *Julius Cæsar*, one of his most difficult plays rightly to assess. Critical opinions about it have been bewildering in their variety. The play acts well, and yet we remain in doubt concerning its final purpose. If we take the titular Cæsar as its hero, why is he murdered almost as soon as seen? If Brutus is its hero, how do we explain several puzzling scenes? So hard is the task of determining precisely what Shakespeare had in mind that several commentators have fallen back in despair upon the supposition that originally it was a two-part play crushed into one.

Perhaps, it may be suggested, an explanation can be found in considering the drama's basic situation and in relating it to another, and more powerful, later tragedy. In *Julius Cæsar* what fundamentally confronts us is the assassination of a ruler, the head of a state, and the consequences of that act. At once, when the core of the drama is stated in such a manner, *Macbeth* comes to our minds: the central theme in both is the same, and, however much Duncan may differ from Cæsar and Macbeth from Brutus, the connexion is self-evident. Nor is this all. Once we recognize the connexion, a certain atmosphere in the one drama begins to lose its own characteristic shape and become assimilated with the atmosphere of the other. As Brutus stands reflecting:

> Since Cassius first did whet me against Cæsar,
> I have not slept.
> Between the acting of a dreadful thing
> And the first motion, all the interim is
> Like a phantasma or a hideous dream.
> The genius and the mortal instruments
> Are then in council, and the state of man,
> Like to a little kingdom, suffers then
> The nature of an insurrection—

it is almost Macbeth's voice we hear.

Let us suppose, then, that *Julius Cæsar* and *Macbeth* were born both out of one essential compelling desire—to write a play, based on one of the cardinal concepts of the histories, and yet different from those, more cosmic in its implications. Let us call this vision the destroying of human order and the infinite woes that follow, the letting loose of evil in the world. If we imagine such a vision tormenting Shakespeare's mind and imperiously demanding expression in theatrical form, if we think of him searching about for an appropriate plot, we can readily appreciate that the theme of Julius Cæsar might, at first glance, well appear to him an ideally fitting story. Let us suppose that Shakespeare thus seized upon it and set to work.

Immediately, the difficulties may be realized. The story of Cæsar and Brutus, both because of its widespread familiarity and because of its treatment by Plutarch, at once set limits on the playwright and ordered for him a course impossible to alter.

What Shakespeare required was an image of order
and a destroyer of that image. Brutus, however,
could not be made other than he had been, a noble
Roman with 'a general honest thought', and clearly
such a man needed motivation in his victim before
he would act. Consequently, neither could Cæsar
be permitted the full scope which might have been
expected of so mighty a person nor could he be
allowed to stand simply as a symbol.

If this supposition is correct, then Shakespeare's
struggles with his material—or, rather, the conflict
between the inspiring vision and the material he has
imposed on himself—become clear. Brutus, a man
with an 'honest thought', needs both the spur of
Cassius and some incentive from Cæsar before he
can be persuaded to proceed to murder. Shakespeare might have taken a cue from Plutarch and
stressed Cæsar's dictatorial qualities, but that would
have meant the writing of a different kind of drama
from that which his inspiring vision demanded; the
image of order would have been an image of tyranny.
Noticeable is the fact that, so far from taking any
such cue from Plutarch, the dramatist has given
Brutus a Macbeth-like speech (the speech which so
sorely troubled Coleridge) in which Cæsar's virtues
are emphasized. Brutus has 'no personal cause to
spurn at him'; he has not known when Cæsar's

> affections sway'd
> More than his reason;

he realizes that

> the quarrel
> Will bear no colour for the thing he is.

Cæsar has not been shown acting tyrannically, and, in view of Shakespeare's treatment of kingship, it would be almost impossible to credit that his approving seal were set on Brutus' rather specious argument:

He would be crown'd.
How that might change his nature, there's the question.

In dealing with his Roman material, therefore, Shakespeare is circumscribed; he cannot quite mould this basic part of the plot to his mind's desire. And he finds himself faced by further problems. By exaggerating Plutarch's account of Cæsar's physical weakness, so far from lowering our admiration, he excites wonder at the transcendent soul of the man who has surmounted those weaknesses, and he has set the stage for that strong reiteration of 'the spirit of Cæsar' which endures throughout the play. The image of order, destroyed physically by Brutus, lives on. Yet it cannot find any clear concrete human symbol. What happens after Cæsar's murder is that the whole of Rome becomes cast into confusion, and Shakespeare deliberately stresses this in three consecutive scenes. The wild frenzy of the mob causes massacre of the innocent Cinna the Poet—the most terrible episode in the action; Antony, Octavius and Lepidus are shown callously pricking names of friends and relatives for death; and following that comes a quarrel between Brutus and Cassius. By these means the disruption consequent upon the shattering of order is revealed—but two dramatically disturbing consequences result: the first is that neither Antony nor Octavius can hereafter step forward as living symbols of the order that has been destroyed, and the second is that our attention and interest is split between the two strong figures of Brutus and Cassius. Because, and only because, there is absent any living symbol of the order restored by Brutus' death, some critics have taken the last lines of the play as a benediction spoken over the corse of a fallen hero; yet the lines themselves are clear. Brutus was an honest man, deserving respect; nevertheless, he was a criminal, an assassin, a conspirator, the killing of whom gives excuse for the drama's last three words—'this happy day'.

One cannot but believe that Shakespeare came to realize that, however well *Julius Cæsar* might act, the concept he had wished to reveal in it still remained incompletely expressed, and we may easily imagine his spirit being fired when he found in Holinshed's Scottish history precisely what he required. In *Macbeth* the theme of *Julius Cæsar* takes new shape. In place of Cæsar appears Duncan, an unknown figure, raising no expectations in an audience and therefore a man who could deliberately be converted into a symbol. One of the most interesting dramatic qualities in *Macbeth* is, indeed, the way in which Shakespeare, who knew so well how to give individuality to the least important of his stage persons, has consciously refused to allow Duncan to become an individual. He is there before us simply as an image, praised in angelic terms; because our human sympathies have not been aroused, we are free to look upon his murder without pity and to view in that murder the destruction of the abstract good. Similarly Brutus becomes Macbeth, and Cassius Lady Macbeth. Here the advantages are obvious. Not only does the marital relationship give a unity to this pair denied to Brutus and Cassius, but, more importantly, Shakespeare can let the Cassius-figure, Lady Macbeth, fade out of the play when her dramatic function is done. And, correspondingly, there comes the opportunity of building up in Malcolm that symbol of returning order which *Julius Cæsar* lacked. Like Duncan, Malcolm appears before us, not as a man, but as the concrete image of an idea.

In *Julius Cæsar* Shakespeare had been bound by the historical events; amid the swirling mists of this antique Scottish legend of Macbeth he has been given the opportunity of allowing his imagination sovereign sway. His original vision seems to have been cosmic in its scope, and here, in *Macbeth*, he can give to the presentation of evil that questioning mystery which its very being requires. The double vision already apparent in many of his earlier plays is now being carried into still further regions. All is doubt and nothing certain—save the ineffaceable confidence in ultimate good. The tragedy speaks to us in riddles based on paradox—from the verbal 'fair is foul' and 'lost and won', through the puzzle of Macbeth's motivation for the crime, to the final metaphysical mystery.

II

By the time that Shakespeare wrote *Macbeth* he had no doubt given his final revisions to *Hamlet*— that drama which above all has captured universal admiration and in which his concept of the tragic has been so completely expressed. Among some modern critics the fashion has grown of pointing to

*Hamlet's* artistic defects; but such a fashion, where it does not depend merely upon a desire to affect novelty, is based on a failure to apply the doctrines of Nature and Common Sense. In no other of his dramas has Shakespeare so profoundly succeeded in presenting to us the illusion of reality and in no other has he so poignantly seized upon our sympathies. The very imagery and flow of words given to the various characters are indicative of the way in which the dramatist has stepped into their persons and become their mouthpiece. Hamlet's own classical imagery appears on no other lips, and his trick of pouring forth a flood of synonyms, as though his mind in the frenzy of its passion had failed to find precisely the word to express his concept, markedly contrasts with Claudius' diplomatically rounded repetitions. Hamlet will rush forth impetuously with—

> 'Tis not alone my inky cloak, good mother,
> Nor customary suits of solemn black,
> Nor windy suspiration of forc'd breath,
> No, nor the fruitful river in the eye,
> Nor the dejected haviour of the visage,
> Together with all forms, moods, shapes of grief,
> That can denote me truly—

while Claudius presents his periods like an official document:

> Though yet of Hamlet our dear brother's death
> The memory be green, and that it us befitted
> To bear our hearts in grief, and our whole kingdom
> To be contracted in one brow of woe,
> Yet so far hath discretion fought with nature
> That we with wisest sorrow think on him
> Together with remembrance of ourselves.

> Therefore our sometime sister, now our queen,
> Th' imperial jointress to this warlike state,
> Have we, as 'twere with a defeated joy,
> With an auspicious and a dropping eye,
> With mirth in funeral, and with dirge in marriage,
> In equal scale weighing delight and dole,
> Taken to wife.

Concerning *Hamlet* a greater debate has raged than concerning any other of Shakespeare's plays; and yet few spectators, now or in the past, have found themselves seriously perplexed by the problems which scholars have found in the text. 'I will hear that play', says Theseus in *A Midsummer Night's Dream*,

> For never anything can be amiss
> When simpleness and duty tender it.

Perhaps this ought to be our motto as well: sometimes indeed we may even get the impression that Shakespeare's purposes reveal themselves more potently to the simple of heart than to the intellectually acute. What ordinary spectators, when left to themselves, derive from *Hamlet* is a series of strong impressions. First comes an admiration for the man, the soldier, scholar, courtier: they see Hamlet as a worthy person, courageous, penetrating and adorned with grace. At the same time, they see this man as one of themselves—greater maybe than any person of their acquaintance, yet not removed in quality from that with which they are familiar. They see him, too, in a variety of relationships and recognize the familiar nature of these relationships. Every man has associations with individual friends and enemies,

with his family, with his society and with his God.
Hamlet alone among the tragic heroes appears in all
these associations. He has his friend, his mistress and
his enemy; he has his dead father, still present in his
mind, and his mother; through Fortinbras and other
characters we are never permitted to forget his
position in political life; from his first encounter with
the Ghost to the end of the play he is set in contact
with the world beyond the reach of human ken.
Ordinary spectators never are really puzzled by
Hamlet's much publicized 'delay', partly because
Shakespeare has adroitly made no delay seem present, and partly, perhaps largely, because they
recognize in Hamlet's relationship to his environment an experience common to most men. On our
initiation into the great world we are all in diverse
ways confronted by the shock of the unexpected and
the hitherto unimagined, and all of us, no matter
how unintellectual or unintrospective we may be,
find ourselves on occasion baffled by circumstance
and incapable of making immediate decisions.

It almost looks as though the ordinary spectators
are right. Appreciated emotionally, the inconsistencies in Hamlet become no more serious than the inconsistencies which real life continually presents to
us; and *Hamlet*'s greatness, its appeal beyond the
limits of time and place, depend upon Shakespeare's
lucky skill in discovering a type of character so
widely disseminated among the races of humanity
and in revealing that character in so many diverse
aspects. Hamlet is Shakespeare's Everyman; his
tragedy is Shakespeare's *Humana Commedia*.

For *Othello*, choice of theme has been made nearer
home, but oftentimes the nearer home we go in

tragedy the farther we travel from our objective. No one denies that *Othello* is a magnificent play, but we may well question whether it reaches the depths revealed in *Macbeth, Hamlet* and *Lear.* What impelled Shakespeare to select Cinthio's tale of 'The Moor of Venice' for dramatic treatment we shall, of course, never know; but undoubtedly it is of interest and of significance that this story expresses a basic theme which appears in diverse forms no less than four times among the dramatist's works. In *Much Ado About Nothing* a bride-to-be, calumniated by a villainous Don John, is cast off, pretends to have died and returns in the guise of her own supposed cousin; the whole tone of the comedy is based on deception. *Cymbeline* introduces a young wife, whose husband, trusting to the tale told him by his friend Iachimo, plots her death—which she escapes through a trick, returning in the guise of a page. Here, to active deception is added the theme of self-deception, since it is made clear that Iachimo indulges in his wager only because he believes that all women are frail. Finally, the same fundamental situation reappears in *The Winter's Tale,* but with this variation—that the element of direct deception vanishes, all stress being placed on the husband's self-deception; the Don John-villain has been driven from the stage and the Claudio-husband built up into a dominating figure.

Obviously, the story in *Othello* reveals itself as a tragic version of the plots romantically narrated in these plays; instead of escaping death like Hero, Imogen and Hermione, Desdemona is fated to perish, and Othello, unlike Claudio, Posthumus and Leontes, awakens to the truth only when his crime has been

consummated; otherwise the themes are the same.
And not only do they bear an outward similarity
to each other; the concept which inspires all seems
identical. When we look at the source of *Othello* one
thing immediately becomes evident: the dramatist,
with a single major exception, has followed the
novelist Cinthio with strangely meticulous attention.
The exception, because of this, assumes peculiar
significance, and we may well believe that it provides
a clue to Shakespeare's own attitude towards the
characters and the events. With apparent delibera-
tion he makes Othello and Desdemona themselves
responsible for deception, thus bringing them into
association with the arch-deceiver Iago. Their love-
making and even their marriage have been so
secretively planned and executed that the bride's
own father at first refuses to credit the truth. That
such a deviation from the prose narrative was indeed
deliberate seems proved definitely by several scenes,
in especial by Brabantio's ominous warning to
Othello:

> Look to her, Moor, if thou hast eyes to see;
> She has deceived her father, and may thee.

As in the two later romances, this direct deception,
shown actively in Iago's machinations and implied
in the secret marriage theme, is here united with a
strong element of self-deception. Othello does not
look at life squarely; his view of men and of women is
coloured by a romantic ideal. Desdemona, as
becomes perfectly obvious in her final conversation
with Emilia, refuses to face realities; her assertion,
'I do not think there is any such woman', is as
romantically false as Othello's idealism. And when

we look at Iago, we realize that not for nothing does he bear a name so similar to that of Iachimo; his judgement of men and women equally depends on the imposition of an erroneous idea upon actuality. Where Desdemona thinks no wife can be false, Iago believes all wives libidinous; in neither concept, clearly, lies a true and objective assessment of reality.

While the exploitation of this theme of deception and self-deception offers opportunity for the creation of powerful theatrical scenes and while the action of *Othello* has been enriched with sweeping surges of verse hardly equalled in any other play, we may be allowed to question whether it affords Shakespeare the fullest opportunity for the development of what he characteristically had to give. In this tragedy the element of the supernatural has been deliberately eschewed and the whole atmosphere of the action rendered domestic. *Othello* might indeed almost be thought of as pointing towards the theatre of Ibsen, and the finest in Shakespeare is precisely that which is absent in the Ibsen form. His tragedy best inhabits dark stretches of territory set in immemorial time—the rude barbarities of antique Denmark, the almost legendary Scottish past, the vague mythical Britain of Lear's days.

What *Othello* lacks becomes evident when we read or see it in close association with *King Lear*. So vast, indeed, is the conception of this drama of pride and ingratitude that it almost, but not quite, reaches beyond the potentialities of the stage. There was a time when critics could state that this tragedy was incapable of adequate theatrical representation: we, who are better acquainted with the form of the Elizabethan playhouse, know better; but even for the

Elizabethan playhouse *King Lear* strains resources
to the uttermost. The characters just stop short of
being symbols, and the episodes, so vastly different
from the episodes in *Othello* that one might almost
have thought they came from different brains, are
perplexing in their diversity and mythical atmosphere. In this, one of the most powerful of Shakespeare's works, he avoids disaster only by a miracle
of genius.

Essentially the tragic atmosphere of *King Lear*
grows from a contrast between emotion and intellect.
In a sense the same contrast is present in *Othello*, but
here it achieves form in more majestic shape and
the whole of nature becomes involved. The very
elements, rather than the human characters, are its
true protagonists. The stars are above us, we are as
flies with which the gods sport—or is this only 'the
excellent foppery of the world, that, when we are
sick in fortune, often the surfeit of our own behaviour,
we make guilty of our disasters the sun, the moon and
the stars'? That becomes the cardinal question of
the play, and we see the intellectually acute exercising their prerogative of sceptical reason, the
emotional turning towards the mystery of the
heavens.

Although Shakespeare's double vision effectively
prevents his writing a thesis drama whose 'message'
may be patent to the meanest intelligence, there can
be no doubt where his sympathies lie. He is decidedly
not an intellectualist; for him what we call the
'scientific spirit' would have been anathema. The
universe is a mystery, and the macrocosm is in tune
with the microcosm: 'we defy augury; there's a
special providence in the fall of a sparrow. If it be

now, 'tis not to come; if it be not to come, it will be
now; if it be not now, yet it will come: the readiness
is all. Since no man owes aught of what he leaves,
what is't to leave betimes?' In his vision loyalty,
however simple-minded, proves the greatest virtue,
and ingratitude the greatest crime. Loyalty keeps
the spirit sweet, ingratitude damns the soul to
perdition. Mistakes may be made by those whose
intellectual perceptions are not of the keenest, but
these mistakes may be rectified in the refining
trials of life. Gloucester may lose his eyes because
he had remained blind to the virtues of his son and
Lear descend to an inferno of madness because he
had failed to recognize Cordelia's honesty, yet both
move onwards to purer vision than they had previously possessed. Ingratitude, self-seeking, callous
ambition, lust, all these are without hope, without
the prospect of mercy. In general, Shakespeare's
vision views the virtues as associated with age, not
mere age in years, but rather age in time. He senses,
perhaps, the rise of a new intellectualism, the advent
of a sophisticated philosophy, and his final word
rings clear:

> we that are young
> Shall never see so much, nor live so long.

### III

Along with these tragedies, in addition to *Julius
Cæsar*, comes a series of others based on Roman and
Grecian themes.

When Shakespeare turned to classical antiquity,
something strange seemed to happen in his mind.
It is almost as though he went back to these ages of

gold expecting to exercise to the full his capacity for admiration and was shocked to find in them vices and weaknesses akin to those around him. As a result, although all the plays built on this foundation have passages of mighty impact, each one exhibits a peculiar spirit of bitterness. Sometimes, indeed, the passages of mighty impact may seem a trifle forced, as if the writer were over-emphasizing his sense of wonder precisely because an element of doubt had entered into his mind; the obverse of this tendency assumes an almost satirical tinge or reflects a linking, in his imagination, of these ancient events and of things close to him. *Troilus and Cressida* thus has Ulysses' majestic admonitions to Agamemnon and Achilles alongside Thersites' railings; in *Coriolanus* some readers have found a satirical intent and others a mirroring of Shakespeare's own concern over contemporary peasants' riots; *Timon of Athens* falls into well-nigh hysterical confusion; in *Antony and Cleopatra* not a few scholars have seen Cleopatra's character springing from the author's experience of such a woman, and only desperate efforts to maintain grandeur through hyperbole prevent the picture of 'a gipsy's lust' from dominating his design. We may gloze over this or that aspect of these dramas, and yet the impression of strangeness will persist in perplexing us.

Throughout the entire series of these classical plays we are presented with hardly a single thoroughly honest and worthy character. In the other tragedies most of the persons moving on the stage may be petty, mean, self-centred or vicious, but, even if we make no reference to a tortured Hamlet and a racked Lear, we draw comfort from meeting the faithful Fool and Kent or from observing Horatio's absolute devotion. Horatio speaks of himself as being more an antique Roman than a Dane, but this allusion to the virtues of the ancient world only serves to stress the quality absent in the Roman dramas themselves. The presence of this mood is least obvious in *Julius Cæsar*, although even here Cæsar is drawn as a tired and degenerating man, Cassius' mind feeds on envy, Brutus, the philosopher and 'noblest Roman of them all', becomes a conspirator and repeatedly shows how his over-confident sense of superior judgement beclouds his vision, Antony's loyalty to the dead Julius springs largely from his own self-interest. In the other plays we descend more deeply. No single person in the whole of *Coriolanus* can truly capture our admiration; *Timon of Athens* introduces a hero whose prodigality is ridiculous and, although he has a faithful servant in Flavius, that character's rôle becomes only a shadow of Kent's; loyalty in *Antony and Cleopatra*, expressed through the person of Enobarbus, becomes tainted with treachery. For true grandeur and for unstained simple virtue we seek here almost in vain.

None of these are satisfactory plays as plays. They have been revived at times with a measure of success, but none has had a compelling and continuous stage history. Of them all, *Troilus and Cressida* must be deemed the most puzzling. Here is the prime tale of antiquity, the tale which in his youth seems so powerfully to have affected the poet, turned into bitterness. Agamemnon and the Greeks quarrel and revile; Helen becomes little more than a whore. The unsavoury lust of Pandarus, the filthy imagination of

Thersites and the dishonourable cruelty of Achilles rule over Troy and the besieging camp. In vain Ulysses calls the chieftains to a realization of the necessity of order; in vain he inveighs to Achilles concerning the preservation of honour. It is characteristic of this queer play that the phrase so often hallowed by quotation in a virtuous sense—'One touch of nature makes the whole world kin'—should have been applied by Ulysses ironically to a vice—

> One touch of nature makes the whole world kin,
> That all with one consent praise new-born gauds,
> Though they are made and moulded of things past,
> And give to dust that is a little gilt
> More laud than gilt o'erdusted.

It is not sufficient to suggest (as is likely) that *Troilus and Cressida* was planned for production before a sophisticated audience of young men at one of the Inns of Court and that therefore its tone was made thus cynical and lewd. There can be no doubt but that in this drama Shakespeare's heart beats miserably, and that the bitter contrast between Troilus' abject repetition of 'Hector is dead' and Pandarus' wretched epilogue wells up from the inner depths of his being.

*Antony and Cleopatra* finds relationship with *Troilus and Cressida* in that both are love stories, with heroines far removed from the romantic Rosalinds of earlier years and from the tragic Cordelias of almost contemporary creation. In the treatment of this work, however, Shakespeare seems nearly, if not quite, to have recovered the balance so dangerously near to oversetting in the other play. Of late, indeed, various endeavours have been made to elevate *Antony and Cleopatra* to a position equal with that of the four great tragedies and we have been asked to see in it the very finest expression of Shakespeare's genius. The problem of assessment here is difficult. Unquestionably, the language is vibrant with a nervous tension and a peculiar felicity of phrase the like of which can only with difficulty be paralleled elsewhere; we realize that a mature Shakespeare, absolute master of his art, rules majestically over the dialogue. Again and again the words, with a magic beyond the reach of any intellectual explanation, reverberate in our brains, echoing and changing significance as the shadows of their original forms blend with what gave them birth—

> the odds is gone.
> And there is nothing left remarkable
> Beneath the visiting moon.

At the same time, despite this wonder, *Antony and Cleopatra* has rarely had for reader or spectator the same power as that possessed by any of the four great tragedies. On the stage its virtue is apt to seep away, and if we read it straight through it hardly leaves us with the overwhelming emotion which enwraps our minds in the others.

The very lavish praise devoted to this work by some recent critics seems to derive mainly from a recognition of the 'cosmic' quality in the imagery and from the way in which Shakespeare has brought together the opposites in Cleopatra's character and the contrasts in Antony's love. The analysis of Shakespeare's imagery, however, should not lead us to the setting up of values based on the images alone. Imagery, for a poet, is merely a means to an end, and an ultimate judgement must be framed from a comprehensive vision of the whole, of which the imagic content is only part. Looked at in this way, one might well inquire whether the cosmic images in *Antony and Cleopatra* do not appear, at least to a certain extent, forced and imposed upon rather than integrated with the central theme. Take Cleopatra's

> His face was as the heavens; and therein stuck
> A sun and moon, which kept their course, and lighted
> The little O, the earth . . .
> His legs bestrid the ocean; his rear'd arm
> Crested the world; his voice was propertied
> As all the tuned spheres, and that to friends;
> But when he meant to quail and shake the orb,
> He was as rattling thunder.

This Ossianesque hyperbole, taken by itself, sounds mightily impressive, but, when we hear the lines in the theatre, with their context, may we not deem that they owe their being to a vague feeling on Shakespeare's part that, in the presentation of his hero, he has not been able to convey to us the essential nobility of Antony? For Hamlet our admiration is aroused at once, and we do not need to have his praises sung in such a way; even a wretched Lear on the heath, reduced to tatters, remains every inch a king; Othello's grandeur becomes immediately evident; and Macbeth, albeit a villainous murderer, captures our wonder. The trouble with *Antony and Cleopatra*, it may be suggested, and the reason it has hardly ever been truly satisfying in performance, is that the hero and heroine, conceived in essentially non-heroic terms, are encased in a heroism of words which do not integrate with the action itself.

Even less successful on the stage, *Coriolanus* baffles us in a different yet basically cognate manner. Once more an unheroic concept becomes wrapped up in a heroic, even bombastic, covering; and the result is an uncertainty concerning the attitude we should adopt in contemplating its action. Here we find patriotism of the noblest sort so combined with pettiness that, quite justifiably, some critics have wondered whether Shakespeare may not have been intending a satirical treatment of an adolescent-minded general tied to his mother's apron-strings. We are inhabiting a world of stark Roman virtues, yet that world is not being viewed by the dramatist with the awful and almost terrifying aloofness with which he observes the worlds of *Hamlet* or *Macbeth*. He is identifying his own interests with his situations and he is allowing a kind of one-sided bitterness to colour his conception of the theme. The mob is treated with peculiar disgust, the tribunes with venom; if the majesty of Coriolanus' courage becomes tarnished by his pettiness, the nobility of his enemy Aufidius comes crashing down in the final scene, wherein the murder of Hector by Achilles finds its counterpart. No doubt Shakespeare is bound here by the facts of history as narrated by Plutarch, but he gives ample demonstration of his own mood in the reshaping of these facts in dramatic form.

The nadir of this mood comes with *Timon of Athens*. *Coriolanus* presents itself to us as a complete whole, but most readers have felt convinced that the inequalities of *Timon* are of a kind to make us believe the play a broken torso rather than a finished work to which the master has given his final approval. Formerly, there were two chief schools of thought:

one argued that in *Timon* Shakespeare had merely revised an older play by some unknown dramatist, the other found evidence to show that an uncompleted draft by Shakespeare had been furbished up for the stage by another hand. A third, and more likely, suggestion has of late been finding support— that the text of *Timon* derives entirely from Shakespeare's pen but that it is no more than a first, and unrevised, copy of a play he never took the trouble to bring to final artistic shape. If indeed Shakespeare thus decided to abandon his work when it was as yet incomplete, a reason may be suggested in the intractable nature of the Timon story—a story which no skill, however great, could hope to mould into the image of tragedy; but perhaps a still more probable reason is to be discovered in the almost hysterical passion breathed into these scenes. Listening to Lear's curses and imprecations we realize that a true dramatist, completely in control of his fictional world, is at work. Into the mouth of the aged king Shakespeare pours words of a searing power; they break upon us like enormous billows, white with enraged surf, so that we are nearly overwhelmed; yet always there is a consciousness that Shakespeare, however much he may seem for the moment to identify himself with the creature of his imagination, remains greater than the object he has fashioned, and this consciousness brings us calm of spirit. Buffeted and torn, we still are not abandoned or without a guide, because Shakespeare the artist stands like a god above the world he has wrought. In reading *Timon* we feel lost, precisely because Shakespeare himself appears to have moved from Olympian aloofness down to the arena, gibbering with Apemantus and frenziedly blaspheming with Timon. There is an entire difference in tone between Lear's tremendous outbursts and Timon's

> Let me look back upon thee. O thou wall,
> That girdlest in those wolves, dive in the earth,
> And fence not Athens! Matrons, turn incontinent!
> Obedience fail in children! slaves and fools,
> Pluck the grave wrinkled senate from the bench,
> And minister in their steads! to general filths
> Convert o' th' instant, green virginity—
> Do't in your parents' eyes! bankrupts, hold fast
> Rather than render back, out with your knives,
> And cut your trusters' throats! bound servants, steal!
> Large-handed robbers your grave masters are,
> And pill by law; maid, to thy master's bed—
> Thy mistress is o' the brothel! son of sixteen,
> Pluck the lined crutch from thy old limping sire,
> With it beat out his brains!

In *King Lear* we have the Fool, an exquisitely imagined creation; his penetrating pathos and loyalty are supplanted here by Apemantus' foul-mouthed pride. Here the theme of ingratitude, a theme peculiarly close to Shakespeare, burgeons forth into monstrous and uncontrolled proportions; the poet becomes so wrapped up in his vision that his words become well-nigh incoherent, the calm eyes are grown blind with rage and the even lips tremble.

So powerful is this impression as we read *Timon of Athens*, so completely has the majestic grandeur given way to such an hysteria and lyrical abandonment of the poet in his creation as to remind us of later romantic passions, that even the wisest and most cautious of modern scholars has been forced to guess at a serious illness about the time Shakespeare was penning the play, followed by a nervous breakdown. If so, however, the illness was no sudden thing. The atmosphere of all these Roman and Greek dramas, written over a period of years, is fundamentally the same. Love and lust cannot be distinguished from one another; treachery and callousness are rife; an abject, miserable pettiness coexists alongside a heroism about which the poet seems unsure and which requires a kind of overemphasis for compensation; certain characters may be styled noble, particularly in laudatory epilogues, but their nobility seems a thing of words instead of a deeply felt conviction of Shakespeare's. The world that the poet saw in writing the Greek and Roman plays is a world shadowed by vice and ingratitude, and one gets the impression that Shakespeare in his more emphatic speeches concerning order, dignity and human greatness was whistling in the dark.

# CHAPTER VI

# THE INNER LIFE

WHILE the clashing, strident tones of Timon's utterance still batter on our ears, we suddenly become conscious of a strange and sudden stilling of the storm. The world of Greece and Rome still haunts us, but it suffers a rich sea-change. *Coriolanus* and *Timon of Athens* somehow seem near to us and, in spite of the peculiar mood inspiring them, their outlines are clear and etched; now, in the romances that follow, we have the impression of remoteness and of colours washed in with indefinite or indecisive outlines. We move from the realm of historical figures—the Cæsars, the Antonys and the Timons—into another realm of myth and legend. *Pericles* derives from Hellenistic romance material; *Cymbeline* is set in an almost prehistoric atmosphere; in *The Winter's Tale* the idyllic mingles with the classical; and *The Tempest* is a figment of the imagination.

I

Concerning these romances of Shakespeare's later career, opinions have been diverse, and perhaps the best thing we can do is to forget the theories for a moment and look at the plays themselves.

Most unfortunately the first of the series, *Pericles, Prince of Tyre*, comes to us in a text which virtually precludes any sure attempt to determine precisely Shakespeare's part in it. We may suspect that more than has ordinarily been supposed comes from his pen, but proof is impossible one way or the other. All we may do is to take the drama as it stands, remembering that doubt exists, not concerning Shakespeare's association with the play, but concerning the exact scope of that association.

At the very start, a peculiar dramatic feature confronts us. The poet Gower appears as chorus-prologue and the entire action is treated as a kind of theatrical representation of a narrative. The author of the play obviously desires three things—to suggest an extension of the action in time, to keep the audience constantly aware of the fictional nature of the action and thus to provide an air of remoteness to the scenes. The characters move from classical city to classical city—Antioch, Tyre, Tarsus, Pentapolis, Mytilene, Ephesus—but none of the localities has the incisively imaginative reality of Rome, Alexandria or Athens. Queerly, however, this remoteness does not preclude the introduction of vividly realistic scenes. 'Master,' says the Third Fisherman, 'I marvel how the fishes live in the sea', and the First Fisherman answers him:

> Why, as men do a-land—the great ones eat up the little ones. I can compare our rich misers to nothing so fitly as to a whale; a' plays and tumbles, driving the poor fry before him, and at last devours them all at a mouthful. Such whales have I heard on o' th' land, who never leave gaping till they've swallow'd the whole parish—church, steeple, bells, and all.

The brothel scenes have the same quality. When Marina upbraids Boult for his miserable trade, his reply has the true earthy cast:

What would you have me do? go to the wars, would
you? where a man may serve seven years for the loss
of a leg, and have not money enough in the end to
buy him a wooden one?

As a sharp contrast to this realistic element comes
that which gives to *Pericles* its most characteristic
and effective quality. Evil, darkness and distress
hold most of the action in their folds. The play begins
with Antiochus' incest and later shows his murderous
intent. Dionyza allows malicious envy to drive her in
the direction of hell—

> The blind mole casts
> Copp'd hills towards heaven, to tell the earth is
> throng'd
> By man's oppression, and the poor worm doth die
> for 't.

Nor is it only man who is cruel: the elements toss
Pericles, like another Ulysses, from coast to coast,
and although he reaches haven in the end the
impression left in our minds is that of a man sorely
tried and buffeted by invisible forces above and
around him. Opposed to this, however, are examples
of extraordinary human virtue, and the universe,
which sends tempestuous storms on Pericles' head,
can also yield miracles. Thus is aroused in us a
sense of supreme and indefinable wonder. No scene
more fully exemplifies this than that in which
Pericles, near unto death, recognizes the girl Marina
as his lost daughter: 'Give me my robes', he cries,

> I am wild in my beholding.
> O heavens bless my girl! But hark, what music?
> Tell Helicanus, my Marina, tell him

O'er, point by point, for yet he seems to doubt,
How sure you are my daughter.  But what music?
*Helicanus:* My lord, I hear none.
*Pericles:*                          None?
The music of the spheres.  List, my Marina.
*Lysimachus:* It is not good to cross him.  Give him way.
*Pericles:* Rarest sounds!  Do ye not hear?
*Lysimachus:* Music, my lord?  I hear.
*Pericles:*                          Most heavenly music!
It nips me unto list'ning, and thick slumber
Hangs upon mine eyes.  Let me rest.

And in his rest, the vision of the goddess Diana
appears to him, bidding him go to Ephesus—where
eventually he finds the wife, Thaisa, whom he has
believed dead.

This scene is typical.  It suggests the distant,
dreamlike nature of the whole play; it concentrates
on what becomes its fundamental core—the concept
of a return, as from death, to life; and it emphasizes the
impression we have of human beings going their ways
under the constantly observant angry or beneficent
eyes of the gods.  The 'most high gods' consume the
evil Antiochus in a blast of heavenly fire, and the
'most just gods' bring Pericles, Thaisa and Marina to
a calm anchorage.  Constantly, throughout the drama
come scenes when the breathing grows hushed as in
the presence of a mystery.

It is this mystery which impinges on our minds
rather than the characters or the events.  The characters indeed assume an almost visionary quality, so
that they stand before us, not so much as symbols,
but rather as a dramatic excuse for the presentation
of the miraculous; and the action at times is dealt
with so summarily as almost to suggest the crudity of

an amateur's pen.  Leonine, sworn by Dionyza to
kill Marina, seizes the young girl with intent to effect
his purpose, when suddenly, without warning,

*Enter Pirates*

*1 Pirate:* Hold, villain!                    (*Leonine runs away.*

*2 Pirate:* A prize!  A prize!

*3 Pirate:* Half part, mates, half part!  Come, let's have
    her aboard suddenly.

                    (*Exeunt Pirates with Marina.*

For a moment we may well feel inclined to deny
such dramaturgy to Shakespeare, and then an element of doubt enters our minds as we recall how
many things in *Pericles*, although transformed by a
new mood, recall situations in his earlier works.  Is
the discovery of the long-lost Thaisa as a 'nun' not
the same as the discovery of Æmilia as an 'abbess'
in *The Comedy of Errors*?  And are the pirates here
any less motivated than the sentimental bandits of
*The Two Gentlemen of Verona* or the conveniently
kindhearted buccaneers of *Hamlet*?  One wonders,
although the corrupt nature of the text offers no
possibility of reaching an answer, whether this
apparent artlessness, like the studiously archaic
verse of the Gower prologues, may not indeed be
Shakespeare's and either artfully contrived or the
result of a peculiar process in his mind.

II

An approximation to an answer may perhaps come
from a comparison of *Pericles* with its companion
romances.  When we turn to *Cymbeline* we recognize
that we are still in the same remote world and that

the prevailing blank-verse style has the same new
cadences apparent in the better preserved portions
of its immediate predecessor. Listening to Pericles'

> I am great with woe, and shall deliver weeping.
> My dearest wife was like this maid, and such a one
> My daughter might have been. My queen's square
>     brows;
> Her stature to an inch; as wand-like straight;
> As silver-voic'd; her eyes as jewel-like,
> And cas'd as richly; in pace another Juno;
> Who starves the ears she feeds, and makes them
>     hungry,
> The more she gives them speech—

we easily move to the opening words of *Cymbeline*:

> *1 Gentleman:* You do not meet a man but frowns. Our
>     bloods
> No more obey the heavens than our courtiers
> Still seem as does the king.
> *2 Gentleman:*                    But what's the matter?
> *1 Gentleman:* His daughter, and the heir of 's kingdom,
>     whom
> He purpos'd to his wife's sole son (a widow
> That late he married), hath referr'd herself
> Unto a poor but worthy gentleman. She's wedded;
> Her husband banish'd; she imprison'd. All
> Is outward sorrow, though I think the king
> Be touch'd at very heart.

There is here the same story-book atmosphere:
Imogen's wicked stepmother steps right out of a
fairy-tale, and the wild cave-life of Guiderius and
Arviragus wanders in from medieval romance. The
juxtapositions are equally abrupt and apparently

naïve. Nature, that gave Cerimon his magical power, works just as magically for Guiderius and Arviragus; solemn music sounds and visionary figures circle round Posthumus as he lies sleeping; the seemingly dead Imogen, over whose supposed corse is sung that exquisite dirge,

> Fear no more the heat o' the sun,

is brought back to life. Older material has, too, been introduced and reworked in this play. The general early British atmosphere reminds us of *King Lear*; Iachimo is another, though lesser Iago, Posthumus an Othello and Imogen a Desdemona; and, in a rather strange manner, even motifs from the very early *Titus Andronicus* enter in to take new shape.

With *Cymbeline* we are on surer ground than we are with *Pericles*. Reading the latter, we can never be sure whether peculiarities in the action and in the style may not be due to textual corruption or to collaborative effort; but *Cymbeline*, even although some editors have needlessly suspected the inclusion in it of non-Shakespearian material, may be taken as authentic. We are in a position, therefore, to judge precisely what the author aimed to accomplish and to assess success or failure. The impression gained from contemplation of the characters in *Pericles* is here amply confirmed. It becomes clear that the dramatist no longer is so deeply interested in character as once he was. With a strange and puzzling fitfulness the dramatic figures come alive and revert into symbols; now they exhibit one quality and now they turn into different persons. Imogen has life in some scenes; in others she shows herself a mere puppet. Cloten at one moment is a boorish clown and at another a patriotic, nobly spoken prince.

In seeking to determine Shakespeare's purpose here, even in seeking to determine whether he had a purpose at all, a strange thought may come to us. When we think of the atmosphere and style of *Pericles* and *Cymbeline* we are almost inevitably reminded of the atmosphere and style of the last dramas written by Bernard Shaw. There is remarkable similarity between them. In both, the authors have ranged over their own earlier works, refashioning older scenes and characters. The same fitful quality is apparent, passages of dramatic appeal being associated with evident crudities. While in neither does the strength of verbal utterance suffer impairment, each shows a waning power in the presentation of a centralizing concept. And, above all, we gain the impression that for both dramatists the plays they were thus writing towards the end of their careers at once reflected something of a new experience and was more closely bound than most of their earlier plays had been to personal emotions.

If this parallel has any validity, it would seem to suggest that, while Shakespeare's power over words remained peerless, some change had come upon him which interfered with his previous interest in character and which permitted him to introduce into these latest works inequalities of a disturbing kind. We can hardly dismiss these dramas as the careless efforts of a man bored with the stage; rather we feel that the author's mind has become so dominated by two things—the sense of wonder and the sense of the unreality of reality—that he becomes incapable of paying such close attention to the niceties of dramatic structure as he had done in his earlier works. The carelessness is not the result of boredom but rather due to a combination of failing structural power and of intentness on something other than action and character.

Both of the two dominating concepts had already been largely exploited in Shakespeare's earlier plays, so that we are not encountering something entirely new, but both are expressed here, not so much with a greater sense of urgency, as with a more profound, if groping, sense of the mysterious. Looking at the earlier manifestations of this mood, we realize that it is dangerous, as some have done, to trace its appearance here to a deep personal experience on the author's part, yet the very insistence on the mood itself, associated with the peculiar dramaturgy and the style, suggests some close connexion between the plays and the writer's own emotions. The words 'dream' and 'vision' so descend upon us in echoing repetition that no other course is open to us but to presume the basic cause of these plays' composition to be a vivid wonder at the mysterious interweaving of dream and reality, at the god-encircled life of man and at the power of the miraculous in the affairs of the world.

III

*Cymbeline* and *Pericles*, both entitled, like the tragedies, with the names of their central characters, are 'tragic' essays in the expression of this mood: in *The Winter's Tale* and *The Tempest* comedy begins to rule—almost as though Shakespeare, after having passed through a period of solemn awe when no more than a hint of laughter would have been appropriate, had recaptured his old serenity, made richer by this deep experience.

*The Winter's Tale* stresses in its very title the fictional nature of the action, and the repetition of the phrase 'like an old tale' keeps the audience constantly aware of this. The extension in time provided by the narrational method carries the plot over a period of sixteen years, and Time, so far from having an 'inaudible and noiseless foot', struts in person on the stage. In all essential respects, the spirit of this play corresponds with the spirit of *Pericles* and *Cymbeline*, yet now the evil which had dominated in these has completely evaporated. There is not a single vicious person in the whole of the plot; even Leontes' jealousy, akin to the jealousy of Posthumus, is provided with no motivating Iachimo.

Clearly, Shakespeare's turning from a would-be tragic atmosphere made happy in the end to a genuinely comic atmosphere with tragic overtones was much better suited to his purpose, and *The Winter's Tale* may be esteemed one of his most successful plays. Yet it exhibits precisely the same apparent *naïvetés* as the others. The characters are endowed with a trifle more of life, but they still can shift their natures and indulge in wholly unmotivated actions. Equally 'artificial' is the handling of some individual scenes, although now the inequalities may be accepted more easily because the author himself has been able to move from a somewhat humourless solemnity to a smiling certainty. The world of the dream and the vision remains still potent, and at moments we are made suddenly conscious of the ominous sweeping of the wings of the gods. Cleomenes and Dion return from the oracle and refer in awed tones of crystal wonder to its marvels:

*Cleomenes:* The climate's delicate; the air most sweet;
  Fertile the isle; the temple much surpassing
  The common praise it bears.
*Dion:*                  I shall report,
  For most it caught me, the celestial habits—
  Methinks I so should term them—and the reverence
  Of the grave wearers. O, the sacrifice!
  How ceremonious, solemn, and unearthly
  It was i' the offering!
*Cleomenes:*           But, of all, the burst
  And the ear-deafening voice of the oracle,
  Kin to Jove's thunder, so surprised my sense
  That I was nothing.

Generally, however, in *The Winter's Tale* the impression we receive is of a poet who, although he has become almost incapable of disassociating in his mind the dream from the reality, yet preserves what can only be called a humorous attitude—as though he were half prepared to believe his fancies idle. Autolycus, though bearing the name of a thievish god, is of the earth earthy, and his cheery, if disreputable, presence keeps us from veering too far away from the tangible. Through him we are kept aware that Perdita's idyllic garden is bounded by ordinary hedgerows on which hangs washing apt for his nefarious hands.

Perhaps the most informative scene in the whole play is the most notorious—that where Antigonus, bearing the baby Perdita, and a Mariner step on

Bohemia's non-existent sea-coast. It opens naturally enough:

*Antigonus:* Thou art perfect then, our ship hath touch'd upon
　The deserts of Bohemia?
*Mariner:*　　　　　　　　　Ay, my lord, and fear
　We have landed in ill time. The skies look grimly
　And threaten present blusters. In my conscience
　The heavens with that we have in hand are angry
　And frown upon 's.
*Antigonus:* Their sacred wills be done! Go get aboard;
　Look to thy bark. I'll not be long before
　I call upon thee.
*Mariner:* Make your best haste, and go not
　Too far i' th' land. 'Tis like to be loud weather.
　Besides, this place is famous for the creatures
　Of prey that keep upon 't.
*Antigonus:*　　　　　　　Go thou away;
　I'll follow instantly.

Then suddenly we move into another sphere. Antigonus, standing alone, gives utterance to a long soliloquy:

　Come, poor babe.
　I have heard, but not believ'd, the spirits o' th' dead
　May walk again. If such thing be, thy mother
　Appear'd to me last night; for ne'er was dream
　So like a waking. To me comes a creature,
　Sometimes her head on one side, some another;
　I never saw a vessel of like sorrow,
　So fill'd and so becoming. In pure white robes,
　Like very sanctity, she did approach
　My cabin where I lay; thrice bow'd before me;
　And, gasping to begin some speech, her eyes
　Became two spouts. The fury spent, anon

Did this break from her: 'Good Antigonus,
Since fate, against thy better disposition,
Hath made thy person for the thrower-out
Of my poor babe, according to thine oath,
Places remote enough are in Bohemia,
There weep and leave it crying; and, for the babe
Is counted lost for ever, Perdita
I prithee call 't. For this ungentle business,
Put on thee by my lord, thou ne'er shalt see
Thy wife Paulina more.' And so, with shrieks
She melted into air. Affrighted much,
I did in time collect myself, and thought
This was so and no slumber. Dreams are toys:
Yet, for this once, yea, superstitiously,
I will be squared by this. I do believe
Hermione hath suffer'd death—

The speech has an obvious artificiality, and, it would seem, this artificiality is deliberately introduced to harmonize with the famous 'Exit, pursued by a bear'. The vision itself, however, has been put forward as a real one; its prophecy comes true, and it is as though Antigonus perishes because of his own lack of faith. Hermione is not dead; the visionary 'creature' he saw in his dream was a figment of the gods. Immediately thereafter, a third note is sounded. An Old Shepherd enters, grumbling:

I would there were no age between ten and three-and-twenty, or that youth would sleep out the rest; for there is nothing in the between but getting wenches with child, wronging the ancientry, stealing, fighting.

And beyond this we go, when the Clown, his son, comes in to report a shipwreck and Antigonus' end:

And then for the land-service,—to see how the bear tore out his shoulder-bone; how he cried to me for help,

and said his name was Antigonus, a nobleman:—but
to make an end of the ship,—to see how the sea flap-
dragon'd it:—but first, how the poor souls roar'd, and
the sea mockt them;—and how the poor gentleman
roar'd, and the bear mocked him, both roaring louder
than the sea or weather.

*Shepherd:* Name of mercy, when was this, boy?

*Clown:* Now, now; I have not winkt since I saw these
sights; the men are not yet cold under water, nor the
bear half-dined on the gentleman—he's at it now.

Perdita is brought from death to life under the
watchful eyes of the gods, amidst death and uproar-
ious laughter. 'Now bless thyself', says the Shepherd
'Thou met'st with things dying, I with things new-
born'—and, as the Clown departs to bury the
remains of Antigonus, 'Tis a lucky day, boy, and
we'll do good deeds on't.'

Various attempts have recently been made to
treat *Pericles*, *Cymbeline* and *The Winter's Tale*
symbolically or allegorically, but it may well be
questioned whether such attempts are justifiable.
Of symbols, no doubt, there are many, and no one
would be so hazardous as to deny that the tempest in
the first play and the disastrous shipwreck in the
third did not have an imaginative significance for
Shakespeare's mind. To go much farther, however,
is dangerous: there does not seem to be here any
clearly worked out and meticulous allegorical content, every part capable of interpretation. Rather,
we are confronted by plays wherein the author,
remembering situations with which he had already
dealt, utilizes them again under the impress of a new
mood. Hero's return is reborn in the return of
Hermione, and Othello reshaped in Leontes.

At the same time, not logically but imaginatively, Shakespeare's mind obviously is occupying itself with what may be called philosophical questions, and in particular he is concerned with the eternal problem of the relationship between primitive simplicity, nature in its pure form, and man's ingenuity. This theme becomes manifest in the discussion concerning the

> streakt gillyvors,
> Which some call nature's bastards.

Perdita will have none of them since they are creations of man:

> I'll not put
> The dibble in earth to set one slip of them;
> No more than, were I painted, I would wish
> This youth should say, 'twere well, and only therefore
> Desire to breed by me.

'Yet', as Polixenes demonstrates,

> Nature is made better by no mean,
> But nature makes that mean: so, over that art
> Which you say adds to nature, is an art
> That nature makes. You see, sweet maid, we marry
> A gentle scion to the wildest stock,
> And make conceive a bark of baser kind
> By bud of nobler race: this is an art
> Which does mend nature—change it rather; but
> The art itself is nature.

Precisely this same theme occupies part of *The Tempest*. It appears concretely in the relations between Prospero and Caliban; it is theoretically discussed by Gonzalo and his companions. There can be no doubt but that Shakespeare, during these last years, was allowing his mind to range over the problems which in diverse ways had always occupied his attention—the problems raised by a contemplation of the conflict between natural freedom and the laws of society, between nature's creative power and man's imposition upon nature. As in the past, he shows no doctrinaire, rationally developed views; these are poetic intuitions, not thoughts. If Gonzalo pictures a land of perfect freedom, yet he (like Jack Cade before him) would be king over it; if Prospero teaches Caliban language, the only profit to his pupil is that he has learned how to curse.

Beyond this conflict lies a still greater conflict between the sensible world and the world of the spirit. Now the dreams and the visions which had been perplexing Shakespeare in the earlier romances become, as it were, objectified, and in the most famous speech in the play Prospero, speaking earnestly from his great treasure of wisdom, sees all the apparently substantial things of this earth as nothing more than the figments of a dream. The realm of sleep, which had so often and so profoundly impressed the dramatist, enlarges its confines and embraces the whole of life. And yet, so subtle is Shakespeare's art, the Prospero who gives voice to these sentiments contentedly buries his magical book and wonder-working staff, prepared to return to his human dukedom.

Although in structure *The Tempest* deviates markedly from the extended canvas of *Pericles*, *Cymbeline* and *The Winter's Tale*, in fact its planning is not far removed from these. All that happens is that the narrative element so fully exploited in the other plays becomes directly incorporated into the action. Had *The Tempest* been written like *Pericles*, we should have started with a scene in Prospero's dukedom and traced his fortunes until he arrived at his island; we should have witnessed his releasing of Ariel and his taming of Caliban. All of this is presented to us by direct narration, but the effect is the same: here, as in the companion romances, we gain the impression of a lengthy extension of time, even although, in this case, the fictional action on the stage occupies no more than a few brief hours.

Perhaps because of Shakespeare's concentration on time and place, *The Tempest* is easier to appreciate nowadays than any of its companions. The Elizabethan stage more readily than ours permitted the dramatic passing of time and a flitting from place to place, and its bare structure was better fitted than our scenic theatre to bring out the qualities desired by the dramatist. When these plays are revived today they are generally taken as excuses for rich and fantastic visual display; and for this justification seems to exist in what several critics have described as a tendency on Shakespeare's part towards 'spectacularism'. The suggestion, indeed, has frequently been made that here he was influenced by the colour and form of the masque, so enthusiastically being cultivated at court by Inigo Jones. While the influence of the masque may be conceded, what we should never forget is that the spectacularism in the romances is implied rather than stated; it is a spectacularism of the imagination rather than of reality. When we think of such productions as *Pericles* at Stratford in 1948 and *The Tempest* at the Old Vic in 1928 we must realize that the inherent vision which possessed Shakespeare in the composition of his romances can come to us only when the imagination is left free to create in ideal terms the dreamlike background against which his action is set. We must meet mind with mind, recognizing that for him the mental and spiritual has come to assume a being of its own. This is being constantly stressed for us. 'Affection!' cries Leontes,

> Thy intention stabs the centre;
> Thou dost make possible things not so held,
> Communicatest with dreams—how can this be?—
> With what's unreal thou coactive art,
> And fellow'st nothing; then 'tis very credent
> Thou mayst co-join with something; and thou dost.

And again:

> There may be in the cup
> A spider steep'd, and one may drink, depart,
> And yet partake no venom, for his knowledge
> Is not infected: but if one present
> The abhorr'd ingredient to his eye, make known
> How he hath drunk, he cracks his gorge, his sides,
> With violent hefts. I have drunk, and seen the spider.

'I think,' declares Perdita,

> I think affliction may subdue the cheek,
> But not take in the mind.

There perhaps is to be found nothing entirely novel in such remarks. Already Hamlet had cried out in agony:

> O God, I could be bounded in a nut-shell, and count myself a king of infinite space, were it not that I have bad dreams.

And even in the early *Richard II* there is emphasis on this theme: the Queen is in despair and Bushy counsels her:

> Each substance of a grief hath twenty shadows,
> Which shows like grief itself, but is not so;
> For sorrow's eye, glazed with blinding tears,
> Divides one thing entire to many objects;
> Like perspectives, which, rightly gazed upon,
> Show nothing but confusion—eyed awry,
> Distinguish form: so your sweet majesty,
> Looking awry upon your lord's departure,
> Finds shapes of grief, more than himself, to wail;
> Which, lookt on as it is, is nought but shadows
> Of what it is not.

To this the Queen replies:

> It may be so, but yet my inward soul
> Persuades me it is otherwise: howe'er it be,
> I cannot but be sad; so heavy sad,
> As, though, on thinking, on no thought I think,
> Makes me with heavy nothing faint and shrink.

The difference lies in the intensity of the concept in the romances. We hardly know how to distinguish shadow and substance here; we often cannot tell which is the substance, which the shadow; and if in stage presentation we make too palpable the one, we may easily lose the other.

### IV

In *The Tempest* many readers have seen Shakespeare's farewell to the stage. Although this notion is laughed at by some among the 'historical' critics, it is hard to credit that Shakespeare himself could have remained unaware of the implications of his own words. No doubt Wordsworth was right in viewing Prospero as an ideal image of The Poet, whose magic derives from the imagination. Yet it should again be stressed that we shall unquestionably be wrong if, proceeding on such an assumption, we go on to make an allegory of *The Tempest*. These intuitions of Shakespeare will not bear rational analysis and their virtue melts away under any attempt to give them precise definition. Shakespeare certainly was not, as some have opined, engaged here in a conscious identification of himself and his life with Prospero and his enchanted island.

If, in fact, this play was intended in 1611 as a farewell to his profession, the farewell was not final. Two years later came *Henry VIII*, in which some critics see the elder dramatist collaborating with the younger Fletcher and in which others find him extending the range of his utterance to embrace new cadences. Outwardly, *Henry VIII* is entirely at variance with the romances in that it emphasizes a realistic purpose: apparently it had a second title, 'All is True'; the prologue begs the audience to think they see

> The very persons of our noble story
> As they were living;

all the facts were carefully taken from recent history. Yet the spirit of the romances remains. Here is presented, as it were, the romance of the Queen under whose rule Shakespeare had been born and nurtured; here, too, solemn music can sound and visions take shape on the stage. If we seek for the core of the play we find it in an almost indefinable impression of the

mysterious ways of God. We sit spectators of in-
trigue and the effects of ambition, of confused purposes and selfish affections, and yet somehow out of
all this dark and troubled world a miracle is born,
the girl-child who is named Elizabeth. Suddenly,
amid the noise and tumult of the crowd, amid the
racy and vulgar realism of their words, a spirit of
prophecy descends on Cranmer:

> Let me speak, sir,
> For heaven now bids me; and the words I utter
> Let none think flattery, for they'll find 'em truth.
> This royal infant—heaven still move about her!—
> Though in her cradle, yet now promises
> Upon this land a thousand thousand blessings,
> Which time shall bring to ripeness . . .
> All princely graces,
> That mould up such a mighty piece as this is,
> With all the virtues that attend the good,
> Shall still be doubled on her: truth shall nurse her,
> Holy and heavenly thoughts still counsel her . . .
> In her days every man shall eat in safety,
> Under his own vine, what he plants; and sing
> The merry songs of peace to all his neighbours:
> God shall be truly known; and those about her
> From her shall read the perfect ways of honour,
> And by those claim their greatness, not by blood.

No more fitting lines could have closed Shakespeare's
career. An Elizabethan, he recognized the majesty of
the time he lived in, and virtually his last words were
spoken in grateful praise of the Queen whose presence
gave him the opportunity for the flowering of his
genius. 'Thou speakest wonders', King Henry says
to Cranmer, but now the wonder, although it exists in
the world of nostalgic memory, has become the real.

# NOTES

[Obviously, any book on Shakespeare, however general, must be deeply indebted to the mass of commentary extending from the eighteenth century down to the present. The following references are designed, not to indicate such indebtedness, but merely to elucidate a few specific allusions in the text.]

*Page*

3 Two typically variant 'symbolic' interpretations of *Hamlet* are given by G. Wilson Knight (*The Wheel of Fire*, new ed., 1949) and Roy Walker (*The Time is Out of Joint*, 1948).
For Charles J. Sisson (*The Mythical Sorrows of Shakespeare*, 1935) Isabella's virtue is heavenly; Sir Arthur Quiller-Couch ('New Cambridge' edition, 1922) is responsible for the epithet 'rancid'.

7 *The Elizabethan World Picture* is, of course, the title of an excellent general study by E. M. W. Tillyard; *The Enchanted Glass* (English edition, 1950) by Hardin Craig is a more detailed survey of the same subject.

17 The existence of certain misdated quartos was demonstrated by A. W. Pollard in his *Shakespeare's Fight with the Pirates* (1917).

18 The relationship of two 'bad' quartos to Shakespeare's first historical tetralogy was shown by Peter Alexander in *Shakespeare's Henry VI and Richard III* (1929), a fuller discussion of a thesis set forth in 1924.

20 On the rightness of the Folio's 'rebellious dead' see H. W. Donner, 'De Dödas Uppror: ett omtristat textstalle; *Macbeth*' (*Acta Academicae Aboensis, Humaniora XVIII*, 1949).

23 The significance of the Folio's lineation in *Macbeth* is well discussed by James G. McManaway in *Shakespeare Survey* 2 (1949), 146–7. Richard Flatter gives theatrical justification for much of the lining in the Folio (*Shakespeare's Producing Hand*, 1948).

44 On the button in *Lear* see Leo Kirschbaum, 'A Detail in *King Lear*' (*Review of English Studies*, April 1948).

47 A discussion of 'humour'd' in *Richard II* appears in Matthew W. Black, 'Problems in the Editing of Shakespeare. Interpretation' (*English Institute Essays, 1947*, 1948, 122–4).

49 Tucker Brooke is responsible for remarking that Shakespeare had 'a humanity so immense that few could note how completely he had failed to be Elizabethan' (*Essays on Shakespeare and Other Elizabethans*, 1948, 31).

52 L. L. Schücking endeavoured to show that Cleopatra was a patchwork (*Character Problems in Shakespeare*, 1922): comment is provided by E. E. Stoll, *Poets and Playwrights* (1930), 1–30. The retention in *Hamlet* of early material is a commonplace among historical critics.

56 The endeavour to discover Shakespeare's personality was the main object in Caroline Spurgeon's pioneering *Shakespeare's Imagery* (1935).

60 The references are to two interpretative studies: S. L. Bethell, *The Winter's Tale* (1948), 118, and Roy Walker, *The Time is Free* (1949), 108.

60 Examples of the evaluations alluded to appear in G. Wilson Knight, *The Crown of Life* (1947), 256–336 and *The Wheel of Fire* (1949), 207–39.

68 Shakespeare's indebtedness to his school-training is meticulously examined by T. W. Baldwin in *William Shakspere's Small Latine and Less Greeke* (1944).

68 The judgement on Shakespeare's learning is that of F. S. Boas.

71 Many scholars, of course, regard *Henry VI* as a composite work; if it were, then the Latin and French tags might be denied to Shakespeare's hand.

75 A recent production of *Henry VI, Part 2* (Birmingham Repertory Theatre, 1950) proved the stage worthiness of this play but the interest of this revival in no way invalidates the general remarks made in the text.

80 Among recent productions of *The Taming of the Shrew*, perhaps that which has most markedly stressed the 'gentlemanly' quality in Petruchio and the comic (as opposed to the farcical) element in the plot is that of Donald Wolfit.

93 On the stage-directions in *The Comedy of Errors* see Sir E. K. Chambers, *William Shakespeare* (1930) i, 307.

111  There is an excellent survey of *The Sources of Much Ado about Nothing* (1950) by Charles T. Prouty.

134  The parallel between *Julius Cæsar* and *Macbeth* was developed independently from an examination of the purely dramatic qualities of the two plays: G. Wilson Knight (*The Wheel of Fire*, 1949, 120–39) interestingly discusses the character relationships between Brutus and Macbeth.

136  See *Coleridge's Shakespearean Criticism*, ed. T. M. Raysor (1930) i, 16.

151  For recent evaluations of *Antony and Cleopatra* see G. Wilson Knight, *The Imperial Theme* (1931), 199–326; J. F. Danby, 'The Shakespearean Dialectic: An Aspect of *Antony and Cleopatra*' (*Scrutiny*, Sept. 1949) and L. C. Knights, 'On the Tragedy of *Antony and Cleopatra*' (*Scrutiny*, winter 1949).

153  An interpretation of *Coriolanus* as a 'tragical satire' appears in Oscar J. Campbell's *Shakespeare's Satire* (1943).

156  Sir E. K. Chambers, *William Shakespeare* (1930) i, 86.

164  That Shakespeare was bored in writing the later romances is strongly argued by Lytton Strachey, *Books and Characters* (1922), 60.

176  J. C. Maxwell, 'Wordsworth and Prospero' (*Notes and Queries*, Oct. 29, 1949).

PRINTED BY
JARROLD AND SONS LTD.
NORWICH

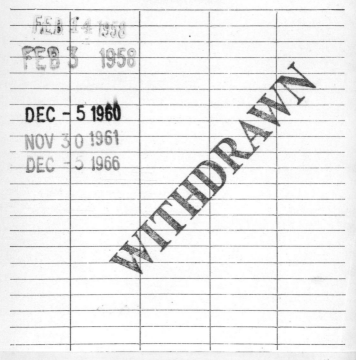